SPORTS
OFF-CENTER

SayItAintSo.com

PRESENTS

SPORTS OFF-CENTER

A TIMELESS SPOOF OF TODAY'S SPORTS WORLD

KEN WIDMANN AND DAN APPEL

PHOTOS AND GRAPHICS BY DAVE LEHMAN

THREE RIVERS PRESS

NEW YORK

Published in the United States by Three Rivers Press, an imprint of the Crown
Publishing Group, a division of Random House, Inc., New York.
www.crownpublishing.com

Three Rivers Press and the Tugboat design are registered trademarks of Random
House, Inc.

Library of Congress Cataloging-in-Publication Data
Widmann, Ken.
Sports off-center: a timeless spoof of today's sports world / Ken Widmann and Dan
Appel; photos and graphics by Dave Lehman.—1st ed. 1. Sports—Miscellanea. I.
Appel, Dan. II. Title.
GV707.W478 2006
796—dc22   2005030138

ISBN-13: 978-1-4000-9795-1
ISBN-10: 1-4000-9795-9

Printed in the United States of America

Designed by Elizabeth Van Itallie and Katharine Van Itallie

10 9 8 7 6 5 4 3 2 1

First Edition

IN LOVING MEMORY OF JOHN AZA LEHMAN

ACKNOWLEDGMENTS

This book would not be possible without the love, support, and critical eye
of Janet Widmann. Thank you so much, J!

Special thanks to the following for their considerable assistance:
Shana Drehs, Daniel Lefcourt, Bill McCarthy, Andrew Stuart,
the International Poetry Syndicate.

We are grateful to Marty Appel, Tammy Blake, Suzanne Brown, Nick Dolin,
Maria Elias, Janel Lehman, Mark McCauslin, Edward Menke, Jennifer O'Connor,
Alex Reinert, Dan Rembert, Elizabeth Van Itallie, Katharine Van Itallie,
and Mike Walfish.

We would also like to thank Nick Dolin, Janel Lehman, Alex Reinert,
Mike Walfish, The Distro, and Edward Menke.

INTRODUCTION

Sports Anger Me

by J. B. GALISHAW
Senior Editor
Sports Magazine The Magazine

L et's face it: You don't like sports, and neither do I. But after being dishonorably discharged from my tour of duty in the first Gulf War, I needed a job, and preferably one that involved railing against things. The Soviet Union having already broken up, there wasn't much left in the world that I was particularly furious about, except countrymen of mine who have it better than me.

I was all set to accept a muck-raking and muck-composting position at the celebrity gossip magazine *Binoculars* when I heard that a floundering sports publication needed a replacement for an editor who had been beaten to death by an angry mob of readers, athletes, and columnists. *Sports Magazine The Magazine* had a long and frequently revised history: Founded in 1931 as an offshoot of the popular radio program *ABC's White World of Sports,* *SMTM* chronicled the athletic

universe with fearless, selective honesty. True to the spirit of its radio forebear, *SMTM* did not acknowledge black athletes until the passage of the Civil Rights Act of 1964. This drew heavy criticism from those who felt that coverage of the Joe Louis/Max Schmeling bouts, for example, would have greatly benefited from some mention of Joe Louis.

Chastened by the backlash from its earlier policies, in the mid-1970s *SMTM* did a full 180, ignoring white athletes entirely for nearly three years. The 1976 Olympic decathlon champion was identified simply as "the blue-eyed devil"; golf coverage suffered mightily.

But *SMTM* found its footing again in the 1980s, as the culture at large had finally come around to a position *SMTM* had held for decades: Nothing matters except money. Black and white were irrelevant next to the almighty green, and from 1986 to 1989 *SMTM* consisted entirely of graphs, charts, and lists detailing the financial side of sports. Not just player salaries, but owner salaries and fan salaries as well. Ticket prices, popcorn stand valuations, you name it. Everything except the games themselves. And complete sentences.

My tenure began in 1991. It has been marked by a switch to soy-based inks, and the hiring of a fact-checker. Also, the rise of the athlete-industrial complex. You know it well—that phalanx of publicists, gofers, and media liaisons orbiting every middle reliever and second-string cornerback prospect.

But that's just pro and college sports, you say, which have always sucked. What about the innocent? Whither those who play for sheer love? To that I reply: Danny Almonte.

He was unfortunate. But you are in luck, because for all their historical missteps, *SMTM*'s "journa-teers" and "repor-tainers" have witnessed every important sweaty event overlooked by the mainstream media for the last 75 years. From Major League Baseball's adoption of "ghost" runners to God's angry press conference decrying video fishing, *SMTM* was there. Or made an effort to attend. Or at least called around to see if anybody knew anything.

Anyway, where was I? Oh yeah: Andre Dawson. When told that the injured Cub was listed as "day-to-day," Vin Scully famously replied, "Aren't we all?" At *SMTM* the answer is no. Day-to-day would be too much work. We are strictly month-to-month. Plus two special issues.

Which brings us to what you are holding in your hand. No, the other hand. You hold a book chronicling a year in sports. Not a single year, like 2006, say. Not a comprehensive year. But a year nonetheless. A timeless collection of sports articles ripped from the pages of *Sports Magazine The Magazine* and arrayed around the Julian calendar. For you, the discriminating sports fan.

In conclusion, yes, winning back-to-back National Magazine Awards is an impressive feat.

It is my hope that day will come.

Enjoy,
J.B.

VOLUME 100, NO. 1

JANUARY

SPORTS MAGAZINE

THE MAGAZINE

Aflac Home Depot Colgate Tartar Control Classic Apparently Not A Football Game

Restless Fans Look For Referees, Players

Despite marching bands and cheerleading squads on the field, fans attending the Aflac Home Depot Colgate Tartar Control Classic in Nashville last month began to question the nature of the event.

After watching two and a half hours of football-tinged promotional activities, Sheryl Reynolds in Upper Reserved Section 36 grew concerned. "You know, it doesn't really say 'football' or 'game' anywhere on here," she said, inspecting her ticket stub. "It's just a string of corporations followed by the word 'Classic.'"

Pausing to whoop along with her seatmates as the roving fan cam approached, Reynolds continued, "And this program they handed out at the gate is filled with roofing tile ads and toothpaste coupons, but I don't see any team rosters."

"You know, it doesn't say 'football' or 'game' anywhere on here."

"And this program they handed out at the gate is filled with roofing tile ads and toothpaste coupons, but I don't see any team rosters."

Although the event was trumpeted on local billboards as "a showcase of America's most exciting teams," assembled fans had yet to witness any live football action. Activities narrated over the PA—a peewee punt, pass, and kick competition; a scoreboard race featuring animated power tools; and a marching band tribute to life insurance—garnered increasingly listless responses.

"I'm sure they're just priming the pump. I bet the game starts in five minutes," contended Matt Finn, in line to receive a free NCAA beach towel by signing up for a Home Depot credit card. "Why would they keep showing all those football bloopers on the scoreboard, and that montage of Keith Jackson's all-time favorite bowl games and shaving products?"

A fan in line at the souvenir stand complained that he was growing weary of being urged to "quack for Aflac." Trying on an oversized foam index finger, his wife said, "And I think we've had to 'guess tonight's attendance' twice."

"The ad in the paper said kickoff 7 P.M.," remarked a woman completing the product survey found in her seat cupholder, "but now that I remember it, I think kickoff was in quotes." ■

O.E.D.: 'Team' Now Spelled 'Teiam'

teethe (tēth) **v.** to grow teeth; cut one's teeth.
teiam (tēm) **n.** **1** a group of individuals who come together for individual glory.
teiam'mate' n. member

Nike Lures Another Teen To Turn Pro Early

13-year old Indonesian seamstress opts for factory job over school, prostitution

> ## "Sure I would have loved to stay in school, if our school had plumbing."

S educed by the opportunity to help her family escape poverty, 13-year-old Jakarta resident Sujatmi Rais became the latest young student to leave school early and sign with Nike.

"This is a great opportunity for me," said Sujatmi, standing on the vast sewing floor of one of Nike's 30 Indonesian subcontractors. "It has always been my dream to buy my mother a home." After signing with Nike, and working 12-hour shifts six and a half days a week for 25 years at the shoe plant, Sujatmi may be able to realize her dream, provided she also qualifies

for efficiency and attendance bonuses.

Speaking discreetly, one eye on the lookout for her shift supervisor, Sujatmi described the thrill of "coming out early," as she stitched die-cut synthetic leather heelcaps onto Rashard Lewis model Air Zoom basketball shoes before placing them on a conveyor belt.

"There was not much else for me to do to earn the money to pay for my grandmother's operation," explained Sujatmi, "unless I wanted to sell myself. So I talked to my people, and turning pro felt right for me at this time.

"Sure I would have loved to stay in school, if our school had plumbing."

On Sujatmi's first day as a professional with the company, Nike officials gave their newest signee the full treatment: showing her around the industrial campus, introducing her to some of her 10,000 new teammates, and pointing out the restroom where she may relieve herself during scheduled breaks. ∎

Photo: © Frederick Balfour/AFP/Getty Images

Own the 100 Greatest Moments in Sportz!

TKO Sports presents the first must-own DVD of the year:
The 100 Greatest Moments in Sportz!
This enhanced DVD is a countdown of the **MOST HISTORIC SPORTS MOMENTS** of all time, **REVAMPED** and **IMPROVED** for a **WHOLE NEW GENERATION** of fans.

"I could never get my 12-year-old, Eric, to sit through Willie Mays's catch in the '54 World Series. Vic Wertz would step to the plate, the pitcher would wind up, and Eric would get all fidgety and complain about the lack of on-screen stats. Plus he thought that the black & white film meant it was a dream sequence. Well, now all of those problems are fixed." —Tom B., Keeseville, N.Y.

Sports has long been one of our **great national heirlooms,** passed on from generation to generation. But in recent years an **unmistakable generation gap** has developed. Times change, not to mention attention spans, imaginations, and basic cognitive abilities. Today's young fans tend to find the "classics" dull, and often confusing. Well, no more. With *The 100 Greatest Moments in Sportz!,* **the future is now. And so is the past.** DVD INCLUDES UPDATED CLASSIC FOOTAGE FROM THESE EVENTS:

BOBBY THOMSON'S "SHOT HEARD 'ROUND THE WORLD" (1951)
• Now **colorized**
• Loads of on-screen graphic displays, including Thomson's "hot/cold" hitting zones and **Ralph Branca's career ERA in road games.**

• Enhanced audio track: "The Giants win the pennant (boo-ya)! The Giants win the pennant (boo-ya)!"
• Commentary by **Jimmy Fallon,** answering all the questions your youngster is likely to have, including "What's a pennant?" and "What's baseball?"

U.S. OLYMPIC HOCKEY VICTORY (1980)
• Through the magic of digital technology, **Russian opponents now North Korean.**

"THE CATCH"—JOE MONTANA TO DWIGHT CLARK (1982)
• Dramatic improvement: original third-and-three play now takes place on **do-or-die 4th down.**

LOU GEHRIG'S "LUCKIEST MAN" FAREWELL SPEECH (1939)
• Background beats from hip-

hop star **Timbaland.**

CLAY/LISTON I (1964)
• Lost footage: over **one hour** of Sonny Liston reciting **his poetry.**
• Ring card girls now with **breast implants.**

GIANTS/COLTS "GREATEST FOOTBALL GAME EVER PLAYED" (1958)
• Now with **TV timeouts.**

JACK NICKLAUS'S MASTER'S VICTORY AT AGE 46 (1986)
• The field Nicklaus defeats now **ethnically diverse.**

76ERS/CELTICS "HAVLICEK STOLE THE BALL!" NBA EASTERN DIVISION FINALS GAME 7 (1965)
• Added halftime show: man in **gorilla suit** performing **windmill jams** off trampoline.

FRANCO HARRIS'S IMMACULATE RECEPTION (1972)
• Includes 8½-minute instant replay review (results **inconclusive**).

SUPER BOWL I (1967)
• **Now with computer-generated sack dances.**
• Never-before-seen lost footage: Willie Wood showering an **unamused Vince Lombardi** with champagne.

KNICKS/LAKERS NBA FINALS GAME 7 "INJURED WILLIS REED" (1970)
• New pregame show featuring **pundits speculating** about Reed's injured leg.
• Reed's two baskets now **thunderous dunks.**
• Bonus commentary: **Stephen A. Smith** on racism.
And much, much more.

Will Montreal Ever Recover From Losing The Expos?

MONTREAL, QUEBEC—The sun doesn't seem to shine quite so brightly on De La Commune Street these days, nor are the Crescent Street jugglers and mimes as joyously animated as they once were. In this charming port city, an uncomfortable truth is on everybody's mind but almost nobody's lips: The magic has been stolen from Montreal ever since their beloved Expos moved away.

When Commissioner Bud Selig announced the Expos' relocation to Washington, D.C., for the 2005 season, the American capital rejoiced in the return of the American game, 34 years after the Washington Senators skipped town and left a void. But another void was left—here, in this bilingual, cold-weather, baseball-crazed city.

"*Les Canadie*—wha? I've never heard of them," said lifelong Montreal resident Guy Legare, 38,

when asked about the local NHL franchise. "The only Stanley I know about is [1977–78 Expos utility infielder] Stan Papi."

In an informal survey, even residents who had heard of the Canadiens and were familiar with their record 24 Stanley Cup championships seemed to show little interest or emotion regarding the team. "Winning gets old pretty fast," explained Guillaume Gouges of the Montreal Historical Society. "Canadians are humble people, we tend to root for underdogs. The Canadiens had a dynasty in the 1940s, a dynasty in the '50s, another dynasty in the '60s . . . by the time the Expos arrived in 1969, the Canadiens were like the 'Damn Yankees'—generally resented by the populace. So this city pretty much ignored their dynasty of the early '70s, and also their dynasty of the late '70s—by that point we had all become 'Expo-nents' and we never looked back.

"Granted, the 'Spos would have a rough decade every now and then. But let us not forget the seasons they genuinely excelled: strike-shortened 1981 and strike-shortened 1994."

But it isn't so much the wins and losses that matter to the throngs of forlorn Expos fans now forced to spend their precious summer nights in jazz clubs and sidewalk cafés, rather than inside a cavernous concrete dome rooting for heroes like relief pitcher Rocky Biddle and outfielder Termel Sledge. No, what they miss most is the intimate rapport between players and fans.

"Les Canadie—wha? I've never heard of them."

"You hear old-timers talking about the close bond between the Brooklyn Dodgers and their fans back in the '50s," said Peter Beguin, 45. "Please. Ebbets Field was packed, there were 30,000 people there every game. You think you were getting chummy with Pee Wee Reese? To those guys you were just a dot in the crowd. You're in the bleachers screaming, 'Hey, Duke, you're the greatest!' and Duke's saying, 'If you want a smile send my agent a telegram.'

"But at the 'Big O' you really did get to know the players. Often socially. I got season tickets behind third base in 1985, and by the following year I was the best man at Tim Wallach's wedding."

"Some people, particularly in the press, like to dwell on the negatives," said Bill Lesourde, 64, season ticket holder for all of the Expos' 36 seasons. "But I choose to remember the good times. Both of them." ∎

Sports Sequels

Hollywood has long believed one successful film deserves another. Sports movies are no exception. Here are some of the film industry's least-known second efforts.

Rocky VII
Rocky v. Bullwinkle

a ROBERT CHARTOFF-IRWIN WINKLER production · 'ROCKY VII' · SYLVESTER STALLONE · TALIA SHIRE BURT YOUNG · CARL WEATHERS and BURGESS MEREDITH as Mickey · director of photography BILL BUTLER, A.S.C. · music by BILL CONTI · produced by IRWIN WINKLER and ROBERT CHARTOFF written and directed by SYLVESTER STALLONE · TECHNICOLOR® · United Artists · Copyright © MCMLXXXI United Artists Corporation · All Rights Reserved

The Pride of the Yankees 2: Gettin' Lucky on the Side (1974)

Who's the luckiest man on the face of the earth? The Iron Horse is back as the Iron Stud Horse, the owner—and extremely well-endowed patron—of a run-down Bronx brothel in this sexy caper.

Brian's Next Song: Still Singin' (1987)

The ghost of Brian Piccolo lives on in this lighthearted buddy-cop musical romp. Invisible to all but his famous friend, now a Chicago cop on the night beat, Brian uses his powers from beyond the grave to help his former teammate solve crimes and sing show tunes. Football musical at its best.

Raging Bull 2: Lovin' Life (1989)

Robert De Niro returns as faded boxer Jake LaMotta. But this time he's joined by wacky, girl-crazy sidekick Reggie, played by Danny Glover. The harrowing, grim emotional energy of the original gives way to breezy one-liners and pratfall-laden double dates.

Rocky III 2
(1995)

Clubber Lang is at it again in this sober, yearning remake of *Rocky IV.*

Rocky VII: Rocky v. Bullwinkle
(1998)

In the wake of successful live-action animations such as *Who Framed Roger Rabbit?* and *Space Jam,* Sly Stallone steps into the ring to fight his first animated opponent in this straight-to-video fiasco.

The Rookie Redux: The Veteran
(2004)

Bleak, true story reveals how dreams can be deferred for years, magically realized, then painfully smashed. Randy Quaid fills in for his brother Dennis (who wouldn't agree to the script) in the gritty denouement to the Disney original, which chronicled the Major League debut of 35-year-old Devil Rays rookie pitcher Jim Morris. In his sophomore season Morris, now 36, allows 17 base runners in ten and a third innings and never pitches in the majors again.

FACES IN THE CROWD

Where we celebrate those who watch those who do

Jon McCauley
KNOXVILLE, TENN. > Football

Fighting a hangover, McCauley successfully held his liquor throughout the entire Florida State–Tennessee game, finally relieving himself in a Port-A-John in the parking lot minutes after the final play. The UT sophomore had been imbibing without release since a pre-tailgate frat party at 8 A.M.

Mary Cela
SPRINGFIELD, ILL. > Baseball

After a close call at third, Cela successfully rallied over three dozen seatmates to flip third base umpire Bruce Satran the bird.

Brent Adkins
GROSSE POINTE, MICH. > Hockey

Season ticket holder Adkins vociferously questioned the sexual orientation of the Red Wings' opponents for the 45th consecutive home game, believed to be a Joe Louis Arena record.

Pete Rose Does Not Belong In The Hall Of Fame

Wasn't good enough player

BY J. B. GALISHAW

It's one of the most controversial sports issues of our time, fueling impassioned debate for over 15 years: Should Pete Rose—the 17-time all-star who broke baseball's cardinal rule against gambling—be allowed into baseball's Hall of Fame? If you ask me, I say no. He doesn't have the stats.

Sure, his supporters point out that Rose got more hits, 4,256, than anyone else in baseball history. But they were pretty much all singles.

And some doubles. Okay, the second-most dou-

> ## Treating every game like a war wasn't just off the mark, it was unpatriotic.

bles in history. And some triples. Well, more triples than nearly anyone since the dead-ball era.

But where's the long-ball clout?

Rose's career highs were 16 homers and 82 RBIs. Was he having trouble seeing the ball?

And it's not as if "Charlie Hustle" was fast, either. People rave about how he ran harder than anyone. Well, if a guy runs harder than anyone but still gets caught stealing a dismal 43 percent of the time, then what does that tell you?

Those same Rose backers always say, "Pete treated every game as if it was a war." Hey, here's a news

flash: It's not a war, it's a game! There are real wars going on all the time, so show some respect, okay? Rose's peak years were during Vietnam; his treating every game like a war wasn't just off the mark, it was unpatriotic.

Betting on his team I can accept, but not a lack of patriotism.

To his credit, Rose did win the Most Valuable Player award once. That's right: 24 years in the big leagues, one MVP. That puts him in the same exalted company as household names like Bobby Shantz and Zoilo Versalles.

Also, Rose played five different positions in his career. Talk about a journeyman! Back in Little League there was a kid who bounced from position to position too. You know what we called him? SCRUB! What did Rose think he was competing in, the decathlon? Musical chairs? Pick a position and stick with it.

In the end I just can't see why so many people want to put this guy in the Hall of Fame. It's probably because athletes who play in big-market media centers like Cincinnati always get overrated.

Look, I can forgive the compulsive gambling—we're all human. But no power? No speed? No Hall. ■

J. B. Galishaw is our senior editor and the author of Overrated: The Willie Mays Story

NHL Struggling To Attract Scabs

With negotiations between management and the Players' Association at an impasse, NHL teams are quietly attempting to marshal replacement players.

"The Red Wings just called, offering a starting job, but I don't know," says former University of Maine goaltender Mike Yarmolinsky. "I'm more into snowboarding now."

"With all the stuff I'm doing," says former Boston University standout Dan Sullivan, "working nights at the shooting gallery, helping my buddy Ray build a half-pipe, and updating my blog, I'm like, 'The Blackhawks? Who's got time for that?'"

"Sure, playing pro hockey might be pretty sweet for a while," attests bouncer and aspiring actor Brian Stegall, who played three seasons for the Corpus Christi Ice Rayz of the Central Hockey League before moving to Santa Monica. "But I'm really focused on getting into movies. Spending a few months skating around on local cable, with a mask on—what talent agent is going to notice me that way? It's just not the right career move."

Responses like these are all too common for San Jose Sharks general manager Jim Goddard. "You'd think the chance to play professional hockey at the highest level would be a drop-everything dream come true for these guys, but we're finding competition from temp jobs, poker nights, and home improvement projects. One guy told me no because he was enjoying working as a chairlift operator at a ski resort.

We are having to throw in heavy perks just to get guys to *try out*."

When Goddard called Lansing, Mich., cell phone salesman and former minor league forward Larry Morano offering a first-class ticket to San Jose and guaranteed ice time with the first shift, Morano considered it. "But I'm a huge Patriots fan, and they're making a run at another title. You think I'm leaving my couch on Super Bowl Sunday to play a hockey scrimmage? Plus, Brady and Vinatieri are going to the Pro Bowl in February—no way I'm missing that.

"I guess it'd be fun to look back one day and say I played pro hockey," added Morano. "But would anyone else remember? Maybe if I played for the Kings at the Staples Center and got to meet Kobe or some Laker girls, it'd be worth it."

For some, current jobs are simply more palatable than the prospect of changing careers. Glen Jonathan, northeast regional sales manager for a copier manufacturer in Manchester, N.H., turned down the Mighty Ducks. "Don't get me wrong, it'd be a real hoot to play in the NHL," he said, "but switching jobs is hell. So many forms to fill out. Not to mention the stress of trying to make new work friends. I'm pretty happy as is." ■

THIS MONTH IN HISTORY

JANUARY 13, 1020— After third consecutive late-season Vikings collapse, Ericsson fired, beheaded.

JANUARY 15, 1975— New "Afro-Turf" playing surface blamed for rise in freak, superfreak injuries.

VOLUME 100, NO. 2

FEBRUARY

SPORTS MAGAZINE

THE MAGAZINE

New Retro Ballpark Harkens Back To Cookie-Cutter Sterility

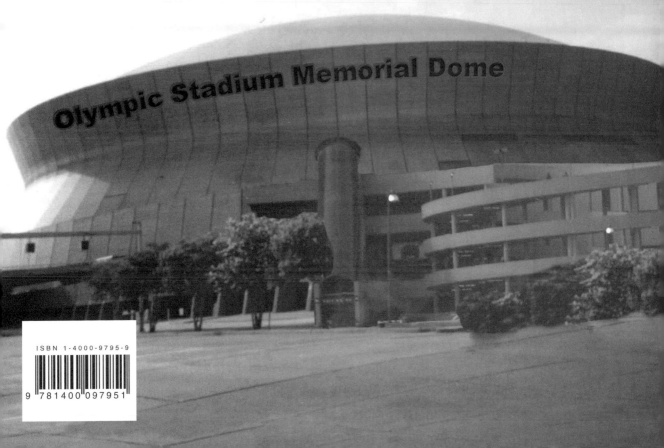

Olympic Stadium Memorial Dome

ISBN 1-4000-9795-9

9 781400 097951

DOME SWEET DOME

HOK Inc., the architecture firm credited with igniting the trend toward intimate, idiosyncratic baseball stadiums with its renowned design of Baltimore's Oriole Park at Camden Yards in 1993, has unveiled its latest nostalgic creation: Olympic Stadium Memorial Dome.

With its fortress-like circular concrete facade, the OSMD revives the bygone feel of 1982 baseball. Fea-

turing symmetrical outfield fences, hard plastic Astroturf, and a fixed roof, the multiuse facility is surrounded by ample parking. A mammoth cluster of freeways—to be completed once adjacent wetlands are annexed and developed—will facilitate traffic flow and discourage public transportation.

Says HOK spokesperson Cindy Hennessey, "We are nearing the end of the line for cutesy throwback parks like we built in Cleveland and San Francisco during the past decade. Today's baseball fans grew up in the '70s and '80s. They remember the Kingdome, Three Rivers, and, most fondly, 'the Vet,' to name a few. They remember sweet summer days spent in air-conditioned chill, and deliciously low-tech exploding scoreboards."

Like its forebears, the new publicly financed megastructure is located in a lower-tax, less-populated region far from downtown. For baseball's aging fan base, it's a trip down memory lane.

Said Hennessey, "It's a baseball fan's dream: pop-ups getting lost in the roof, choppers bounding off the carpeting into left field for easy hits, home runs morphing into ground rule doubles thanks to the overhang-

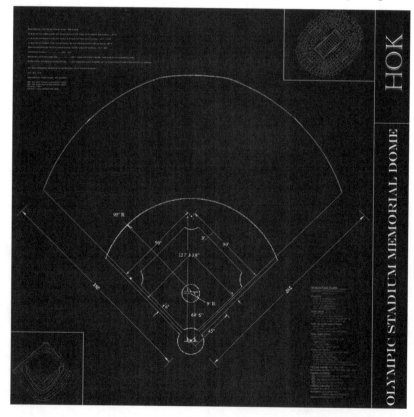

OLYMPIC STADIUM MEMORIAL DOME

HOK

A mammoth cluster of freeways— to be completed once adjacent wet- lands are annexed and developed— will facilitate traffic flow and discourage public transportation.

ing speakers. Most important, 'Lymp-Dome' provides local fans the satisfaction of knowing that almost any event—football game, rock concert, auto show, visit by the pope—could generate tax revenue inside the vast interior, regardless of weather."

"We've thought of everything," said HOK designer Preston Bienstock, "including a garage for the bullpen car. Seatbacks are angled toward the 50-yard line, even during baseball games, and we plan to pipe in disco hits between innings. In design and construction, we spared no expense to re-create the past. At the Lymp-Dome, we want fans to feel like it's 1977, and they don't yet know the dangers of asbestos." ■

Bush Declares Thumb War
Executive Order 1-2-3-4 Forces Kim Il-sung's Hand

1960 U.S. Hockey Gold Medalists To American Public: HELLO?!

The members of the 1960 U.S. Olympic hockey team are not spring chickens anymore. But judging from their annual reunion last month in Boston, their inner fire still burns as strong as ever, and they have a message for America: What the fuck?

"How many movies are they going to make about the 1980 team?" asked '60 defenseman Jack Kirrane. "How many specials on ESPN Classic? How many times are we going to hear the word 'miracle'? I think we get the idea already.

"Meanwhile, mention the 1960 team winning gold and people think you have your facts wrong. We won it, I promise. You want to see my medal?"

A quick Internet search reveals that Kirrane is indeed correct: The 1960 Americans did win gold in Squaw Valley, Calif.—toppling overwhelmingly favored Soviet, Czech, and Canadian teams along the way.

"The guys from the 1980 team still get bags of mail to this day," says '60 star Bob Cleary. "Do you know how many letters I got after we won the gold? Two. One was congratulations from my uncle Marty

A quick Internet search reveals that the 1960 Americans did indeed win gold in Squaw Valley.

and aunt Jill. The other was from a guy who had been sitting behind our bench during the gold-medal game against Czechoslovakia—he wanted to know if anyone on the team had found his glasses."

Bill Christian, another standout on the '60 squad, recalls watching his son David participate in the triumph at Lake Placid in 1980: "To see my son and his teammates duplicate our feat, twenty years later—it's simply impossible to describe the emotions I felt. Mainly, an overwhelming sense of pride. That, and rage. Not one person in Lake Placid even recognized me."

The reasons for the obscurity of the 1960 triumph have never been fully clear. At the recent reunion, several members of the team tried to dissect it, growing more agitated by the minute. Said goaltender Jack McCartan:

"Everyone talks about how '80 was the height of the Cold War, and that's why it's so significant and inspiring. Yeah, '60 was glasnost. It's not like the Soviets had just launched Sputnik. Oh wait, yes they had. And it's not like we'd just been through the McCarthy hearings a few short years ago. Oh wait, yes we had. And it's certainly not like Cold War paranoia had us in such grips that schoolchildren were being taught to hide under their desks in the event of nuclear holocaust. OH WAIT, YES IT FUCKING DID. Give me a break."

Perhaps part of the reason for the 1960 team's obscurity is the media's transformation in the 20 years afterward. By 1980 the coverage of sports had grown far more sophisticated, the creation of hype almost a science. Al Michaels's famous "Do you believe in miracles?!" shriek will never be forgotten. But few seem to remember Phil North's call at the end of the equally historic 1960 U.S./Soviet contest: "Final score 3–2. Thanks for watching." ∎

God On Video Fishing: "Are You Shitting Me?"

God took a few minutes off from business last month to comment on the advent of handheld electronic games that simulate the experience of fishing.

"Are you guys shitting me with this?" asked the Almighty. "What a tragic waste of cranial capacity and opposable thumbs. I should have bestowed those gifts upon rodents, not humans.

"I mean, 10,000 years of civilization? For this? Sitting on the couch trying to land a digital flounder? I made sure the earth was teeming with beauty, majesty, and wonder—not to mention REAL FISH. Get off your asses."

Before departing in a flash of lightning, God added that judging by humans' environmental track record, video watering holes would probably soon be overfished.

Senseless Death Fails To "Put Game In Perspective"

The sudden, shocking death of Randolph High School hockey player Brian Nelson last month has failed to put the game into any sort of perspective for his former team. Nelson, 17, was buried alive by a collapsing irrigation ditch while working a part-time job for a local plumbing company in his hometown of Bangor, Maine.

As Nelson's mud-choked corpse was being prepared for burial, coach Leonard Munn briefly considered canceling his team's next game later that night, before deciding that leaving the schedule unchanged would be some sort of tribute to his fallen left winger. And less work.

Although grief-stricken, Brian's teammates were also unable to examine the event in any meaningful fashion.

"Brian's passing serves to remind us that there are more important things in life. Like hockey."

"The way I see it, it was meant to be," said James Rawson as he reflected on his shift responsibilities while attending his friend's funeral. "Brian's passing serves to remind us that there are more important things in life. Like hockey."

After the funeral, Brian's mother addressed her son's former teammates, telling them how much he had enjoyed their camaraderie.

"When Brian's mother spoke to us before face-off, I thought I was gonna lose it," said center Jeff Boxerman, "but then I remembered that we had a hockey game to play, and I regained my senses."

"You'd think this sort of horrific tragedy would make a midseason game seem pretty trivial," said goalie Fred Cuppett. "You'd think that, but you'd be dead wrong, pardon the expression. No conference game is trivial."

"It's so terrible to lose a friend like that," reflected defenseman Teddy Urso, who had been a classmate of Nelson's since first grade. "It's like when those disabled Iraq War vets came to our game that time. Those guys were missing limbs and organs, and I fucking NAILED that winger into the boards. Sweet Jesus, it felt good to do that for our troops."

In the locker room before the game, teammates discussed wearing black armbands as a tribute to their late friend. Said defenseman Dan Wilcox: "The guys were into it, but then we realized our jerseys are black, so we said screw it."

A rough start against Newtown North caused much concern, but Randolph rallied behind two goals from Robbie Grabel to escape with a 4–3 win. After the game, as teammates high-fived one another, Grabel remarked: "It just seemed like my second-period goal meant so much more, against the backdrop of Brian's sudden asphyxiation."

"Man, what an awful week," mused backup goalie Todd Greer. "The whole thing reminded me of 9/11, when we lost that overtime preseason game to Milton High." ■

WEB GEMS

We scour the Web so you don't have to

Sports Items Seen on

- Kaiser-style pointed helmet worn by Marge Schott to Reds' 1990 Victory Parade
- Hartford Whalers Visa card (Expired)
- Beastie Boys 1986 signature model Wiffle Ball bat
- Tackle Me Elmo doll
- Spud Webb

Lowest-Rated Sports Shows
- *Monday Night Foosball*
- *Greatest Almost-Trades*
- *ESPN's 20 Best Top 20 Countdowns*
- *SportsCentury: History's Greatest .500 Teams*
- *Battle of the Networking Stars*

*Smith Jones, head football coach and business management teacher at Rumson, N.J.'s Hamilton High School,
addressed his squad on the eve of their game against rival University High School last month.*

Sports Coach Uses Business Metaphors

Take a knee, men. Football is a simple game. You block. You tackle. You maximize your returns.

Tomorrow's matchup poses a critical test for this team: Are our solutions scalable? Are they turnkey? We won't know until kickoff, but I'm confident we'll beat forecast results.

Why? Because we're rainmakers!

We've been ramping up resources and closing the quality gap since the loss to Westside two weeks ago. I see lots of improvement around here, particularly in our core competencies: shedding blocks, staying in our lanes, being catalysts for change.

Tomorrow we'll be showcasing value-adds in all divisions—offense, defense, and special teams.

Milic! You're the driver on this one. You gotta upskill your talent. Finish your runs. When you get hit, keep those feet driving. Move the pile! Going forward: I want you going forward.

Tomorrow we'll be showcasing value-adds in all divisions— offense, defense, and special teams.

Macosko! You've got a mission-critical role here. I need you to take ownership of the quarterback position. You gotta believe, deep down, that when the ball is snapped you're gonna monetize our assets. Take what the defense gives you. Find the

---

Slide 21 of 46

Defensive Strategy

- Find the Tipping Point
- Remember *The Art of War*
- Don't Jump Offside

You gotta believe, deep down, that when the ball is snapped you're gonna monetize our assets.

low-hanging fruit. When you see an opportunity for a buy-in, boom! That's when you make an aspiration statement.

Brock, you gotta fight to get open. Upsell the short routes. But pace yourself. Watch your burn rate.

That goes for everybody. If we're backed up in our own end zone late in the fourth, don't start rearranging deck chairs! Just act like it's early in the fiscal quarter and leading indicators have been trending up. Breathe.

As you know, we are taking on a robust opponent tomorrow. Uni High is a major player in our space, perhaps best-of-breed. They have a mature product and an undefeated record. They're gonna say we're resource-constrained, maybe call us "losers." So here's the net-net: This is a golden opportunity for us to gain traction and rightsize those jerks!

We've got a lot of heavy lifting to do, but it's up to us. If we wanna be market leaders, we gotta play like market leaders.

So right now everyone on this team should be asking themselves, "How will I leverage my skill set to help Hamilton win?"

And as you go through the rest of your day— sitting in class, riding the bus home—remember one thing: Talent alone will not lead us to victory, but key efficiencies realized through critical, sustainable synergies will.

Allright men, hands in.

On three, PARADIGM SHIFT! ∎

Holy Shit, Did You See The Celtics Game Last Night?

BY NOAM CHOMSKY, PH.D.

The thesis I wish to put forth here is two-pronged. The first part will be, I expect, no surprise to those who are familiar with my work. The second, however, is based on my most recent findings and is being presented here for the first time.

Part one of the thesis is that spectator sports are a pointless diversion proffered by those in power to subjugate and indoctrinate the bleary-eyed citizenry with a jingoist, conformist, and chauvinist mentality.

Part two of the thesis is: Holy shit, did you catch the game last night?

Spectator sports are a pointless diversion . . .

I am eternally troubled that the public will never be truly free unless it can recognize these gladiator-style events for what they are: mere bread and circus spectacles, insidiously brainwashing the populace while blinding it from weightier concerns.

But perhaps even more troubling is this: If the Celtics keep missing key foul shots, how are they possibly going to make the playoffs? Paul Pierce, you know you're my man, but you're killing us down the stretch. Even back in the glory days of Bird, McHale, and Parish, when we had all the talent in the world, we won because the team knew the fundamentals: Exe-

cute the pick-and-roll, play tough D, and above all: SINK THOSE FREE THROWS. Bird shot a career .886 from the line; none of the current Celtics are even over .800. Free throws decide games.

But on the other hand, I find it truly astonishing that otherwise intelligent people can grow so agitated—on radio call-in shows and the like—about whether the 7-foot-tall millionaires wearing green will deposit a ball in a metal hoop more times than the 7-foot-tall millionaires wearing yellow.

That said, I've been flat-out drooling for another Celtics-Lakers final for years. Payback for '87, Hollywood bitches!

But, I posit, if we as a society remain enslaved to the mindlessly anesthetizing diversion of physical one-upmanship, we will continue to ignore such vital matters as the Darfur genocide.

In the end, it is clear that sports are the true opiate of the masses, fueling an irrational obsession with meaningless spectacle. But ultimately my conclusion, and the key point I wish to emphasize, is this: Fuckin' A, we need a low-post scorer. ■

Noam Chomsky, Ph.D., is a renowned linguist, political theorist, and longtime professor at the Massachusetts Institute of Technology. His more than 100 books include Studies on Semantics in Generative Grammar *and* Manufacturing Consent.

Our recurring feature in which we revisit the sports lore of simpler times, via the *SMTM* archives

Eagles Fans Thrilled For New Level Of Heartbreak

After three straight years of losing the NFC championship game, the Philadelphia Eagles will finally reach the "Promised Land" of having their asses handed to them in the Super Bowl when they meet New England.

"It's a dream come true," says Yardley, Pa., resident and lifetime Eagles fan Bill Kieffer. "All those years losing in the playoffs—now, at long last, we can lose the big one."

Nearly a quarter century has passed since the Eagles got systematically thrashed on the sports world's biggest stage. Having blown three consecutive chances to reach the Super Bowl, it seemed the team was destined to become the off-Broadway version of the Buffalo Bills until they finally prevailed against the Atlanta Falcons to earn a trip to Jacksonville.

As Joe Maple, Cape May, N.J., resident and Eagles season ticket holder, explains, "It's one thing to be a chronic near-miss team. But a near-near-miss? Thank God we can finally take our misery to the next level.

"Granted, we've had some close calls: the Flyers' seven-game loss to Edmonton in the '87 Finals hurt like hell, and I'd say that Mitch Williams giving up that homer to Joe Carter to end the '93 World Series was about as good as it gets."

"I've had my heart broken by plenty of 'Iggles' squads, from the underachieving Buddy [Ryan] and Randall [Cunningham] years to the ridiculous home losses against Carolina and Tampa Bay of recent vintage," says Muhlenberg College student Matt Steinfeld. "But my catcalls and anguished cries always felt a little lonely, like whistling in the shower. When I'm booing Donovan McNabb and chanting for [backup QB] AJ Feeley, I want it heard in 220 countries as well as Armed Forces Radio." ■

Doug Pensinger/Getty Images Sport/Getty Images

VOLUME 100, NO. 3

SPORTS MAGAZINE

THE MAGAZINE

THE WAIT IS OVER! ESCAPE THE WINTER BLUES AND COME JOIN US IN A LAND OF TROPICAL FANTASY WITH OUR FIRST ANNUAL

SWIMSUIT ISSUE

ISBN 1-4000-9795-9

9 781400 097951

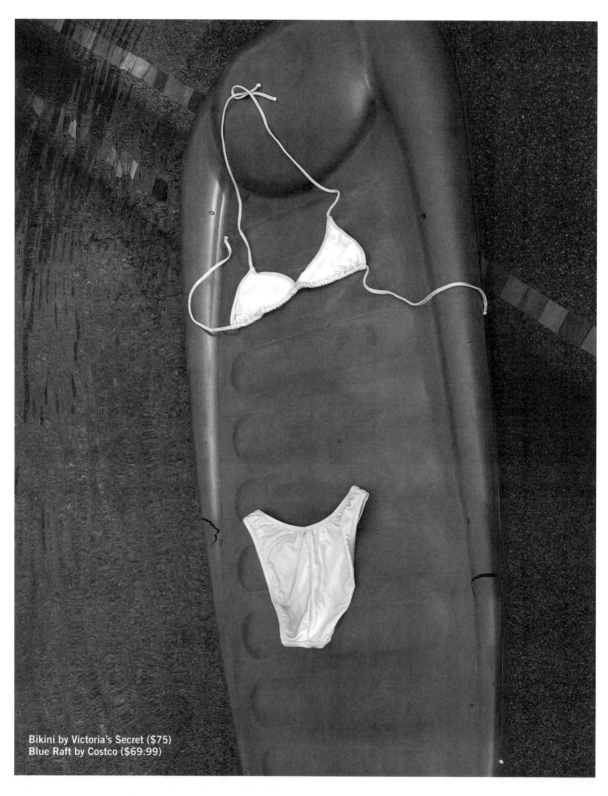

Bikini by Victoria's Secret ($75)
Blue Raft by Costco ($69.99)

Top by Electric
Beach ($65)
Hot Pant by Electric
Beach ($55)

String Bottom by Tommy Hilfiger
($85). Not Shown: Supermodel
Jessica Van Der Steen

Men's Trunks by Old Navy ($14.99)
Towel from Mom's closet (free)

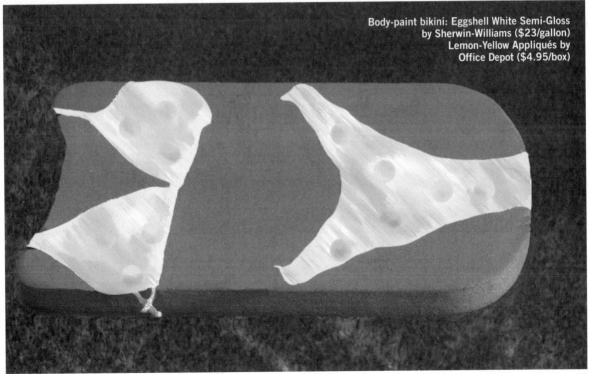

Body-paint bikini: Eggshell White Semi-Gloss
by Sherwin-Williams ($23/gallon)
Lemon-Yellow Appliqués by
Office Depot ($4.95/box)

VOLUME 100, NO. 4

MARCH

SPORTS MAGAZINE

THE MAGAZINE

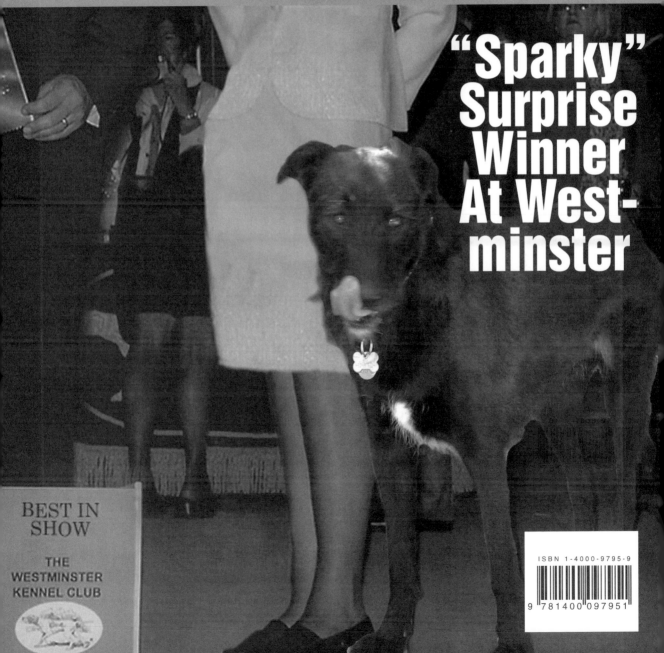

"Sparky" Surprise Winner At West-minster

BEST IN SHOW

THE WESTMINSTER KENNEL CLUB

ISBN 1-4000-9795-9

Shaggy Chewer Wins Best In Show

Stray mutt tops field with insouciant wag, frenzied face-licking

Sparky, a hyperactive mutt that had never before entered a breeding competition, shocked the Madison Square Garden crowd by taking Best in Show at the world's most prestigious canine event.

Said Westminster Kennel Club Dog Show judge Lynette Saltzman, giggling as the black Labrador mix jumped up to lick her face, "He has that *je ne sais quoi* practiced by the rarest of dogs—the ability to surmount appearance, and just *be*."

"I found it an inspired choice," said USA Net-

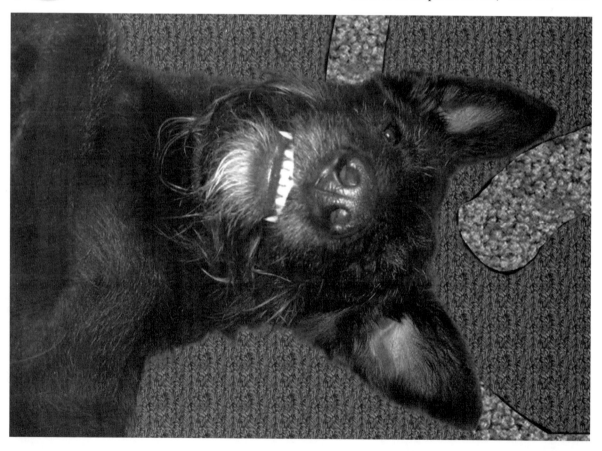

"He just wanted to bounce around and chew things. Pure *joie de vivre.* Spectacular animal."

work TV analyst David Frei while handing Saltzman a tissue to remove fresh slobber from her lapels. "I've never seen a dog so utterly free of competitive angst until I witnessed Sparky nuzzling up to ice cream vendors and scratching himself throughout the day. And the nonchalant sniffing of the carpet during the final judging period! That's cool under pressure, my friends. He's the Tom Brady of show dogs."

As Sparky's handler, Louisville native Marsha Miner, struggled to corral the 4-year-old male after the show, Sparky ran laps around the arena's lower levels, pausing to gobble stray popcorn. Moments later he emerged with a prize: an old tennis ball.

Found in the woods by the Louisville Humane Society at six months, on Saturday night Sparky's black and white streaked mane was heavily matted with what looked like spilled cola. Nonetheless, said Sporting Group judge Paula Nykiel, it was Sparky's refreshing personality that triumphed. "Sparky wasn't like the other dogs—drilled to stand stone-still while their gums are checked and coat examined by a stranger. No sir. He just wanted to bounce around and chew things. Pure *joie de vivre.* Spectacular animal."

Reaction among competing handlers was mixed. Most were won over by Sparky's ebullient wag and broke into smiles as the victorious dog was awarded the title ribbon. A few seemed chagrined.

"It appears that this year poise, grooming, and stacking for the judges mattered not at all," remarked the veteran handler Constance L. Whiting. "I don't mind a healthy dose of impishness, but I watched Sparky chew up a discarded program, and the judge laughed and patted him on the head. Doesn't seem right."

"I thought it most peculiar," said Jeremy Sheehan, owner of the border collie Tracy, who bested the Herding Group but failed in her bid for Best in Show. "Sparky is the ideal of the breed? He spent an awful lot of time barking." ∎

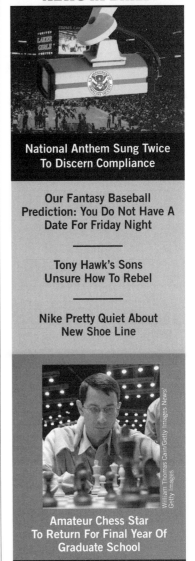

MLB To Promote NBA

$50,000 deal brings basketball to baseball

In its continuing effort to freshen baseball's image and woo younger fans, Major League Baseball has struck a deal to display stadium and on-field advertisements for the National Basketball Association.

Said MLB marketing director Tim Danneman, "We're bringing the in-your-face, dunk-a-rific action of the NBA to the fourth-inning lull. It's everything a true baseball fan could want."

After public outcry in 2004 forced MLB to abort its $3.6 million deal to emblazon Columbia Pictures' *Spiderman 2* logo on bases and on-deck circles for an entire weekend of games, baseball officials insist that this time they better understand the desires of their dwindling fan base.

Explained MLB promotions VP Roger Mack, "When the Spidey hubbub hit, we realized the problem—wrong demo. Our audience wants sports, not

comics. Hoops is hip, it's hot, it's what kids watch today. So there's no better way for us to serve baseball fans than to give them what they really want—basketball."

Terms of the deal—said to be worth up to $50,000 for the struggling national pastime—

> ## "We're bringing the in-your-face, dunk-a-rific action of the NBA to the fourth-inning lull."

include stadium and on-field NBA-themed signage at all ballparks, and basketball-related promotions between innings.

"We will be giving away 2,000 official NBA baseballs throughout the summer, plus hundreds of miniature baseball bats with Shaq's signature," said Mack. "And hold on to your ticket stub, because it just might send you to this year's NBA All-Star Game."

In addition, NBA merchandise will be available at stadium kiosks, and basketball highlights will be shown on the Jumbotron during "Take Me Out to the Ball Game."

Added Mack, "It'll be the next best thing to being at a basketball game." ■

Media Depiction Of Phil Jackson May Be A Distortion

"Big Chief Triangle" allegedly living in teepee

As Phil Jackson approaches 20 years as an NBA coach, the media continue to struggle to understand the Zen Christo-Buddhist basketball guru.

"Has the Lakers' hookah-puffing shaman finally run out of magic beans?!" exclaimed ABC commentator Al Michaels after Jackson's squad lost their fourth consecutive game.

Those who know the coach best insist Jackson, author of *Sacred Hoops: Spiritual Lessons of a Hardwood Warrior,* is slightly quirky and well read but nothing like the mystical sitar-strumming hemp-farmer described in numerous magazine profiles.

Although Jackson owns multiple estates and a wardrobe of tailored suits, *Sports Illustrated* recently reported that he lives on a Yurok Indian reservation in the California desert and subsists entirely on lotus root.

Says media scholar Martin Lacey, "He quoted Lao-tzu once or twice, gave a star player a Hermann Hesse novel . . . now he can't shake this reputation as some dashiki-clad moonman."

> ## "This crazy Buddhist stuff he's always spouting . . . it just doesn't have any place in sports."

And despite the phenomenal coaching success Jackson has achieved, many in the convention-bound world of sports are quick to disdain the Eastern ideas he has occasionally espoused along the way.

Says sports pundit Mike Lupica, "This crazy Buddhist stuff he's always spouting—about believing in yourself, remaining calm under pressure, and uniting with others to reach a common goal—it just doesn't have any place in sports."

At times the comments can turn mocking.

Remarked ESPN's Tom Tolbert after a quick L.A. turnover, "Well, that was a fleeting possession . . . but then *all* possessions are fleeting, right, Phil?" ∎

The Upside To Obesity

America teeming with competitive eating prodigies

The burgeoning girth of America's youth has surprising benefits, says a new report from the Department of Health and Human Services.

"Although some of the effects of the obesity epidemic are indeed troubling," reads the introduction, "it's important to note that, in the international battle for gustatory supremacy, America is in tip-top shape."

The report, commissioned in part by the International Federation of Competitive Eating, holds that American officials should institute a competitive eating outreach program.

"There are 127 million obese Americans—9 million of whom are severely obese behemoths, or SOBs. With a network of eating coaches and a universal set of competitive standards, there's no reason America can't dominate all divisions of competitive eating come 2012."

"To be sure, one does not have to be obese to be a competitive eating champion—witness the success of 132-pound Japanese champion Takeru Kobayashi, who once ate 53½ hot dogs to win the Nathan's Famous 4th of July eating contest. Nonetheless, an increasing pool of ever larger 'eat-thletes' will only bolster American efforts."

Said IFCE chairman Terry Yurdin, "It is no surprise that high-efficiency fat farms like Mississippi and Alabama lead the nation in cultivating chili-eating prodigies. With sedentary populations that subsist on greasy foods like chicken-fried steak, both

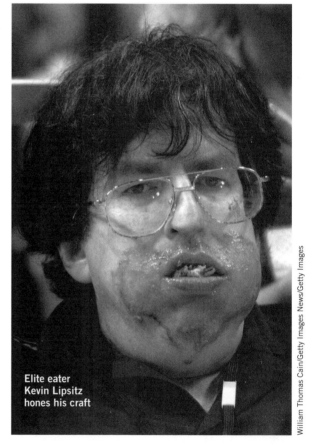

Elite eater
Kevin Lipsitz
hones his craft

William Thomas Cain/Getty Images News/Getty Images

states have obesity rates nearing 24 percent—which make them perfect breeding grounds for America's future champions."

Says East Dover High School competitive eating coach Larry Tribble, "Well, here in Delaware we're playing catch-up, or catsup if you prefer, to the Deep South. We have a ways to go, but we are improving:

"An increasing pool of ever larger 'eat-thletes' will only bolster American efforts."

Obesity is up over five percent in the last ten years. I see good news in other ways too. Forced to find new sources of funding, schools today are way more receptive to selling and advertising junk food. Time was, I had to pull kids out of gym class to shovel down hard-boiled eggs. Now, thanks in part to our 'Just Chew It' campaign, students are carbo-loading wherever, whenever. They can buy Krispy Kremes in homeroom. I've got two true freshman walk-ons— we call 'em 'waddle-ons'—with BMIs [Body Mass Indexes] over 40. Last year, for the first time, I had to ban snacking en route to matches.

"I even had to redshirt two guys this year, on account of no room on the bus." ■

WBO Chairman Decries WBC Championship Belt As "Inconsequential, Tacky"

In remarks that have rattled the worlds of pugilism and couture, World Boxing Organization president Francisco Valcarcel has declared the World Boxing Council heavyweight championship belt "second-tier" and "gauche."

"The WBC belt is a minor league prize," he said, pounding the podium for emphasis at the WBO's East Orange, N.J., headquarters. "It's time for the world to stop recognizing it as a legitimate boxing title, and start recognizing it as what it is: a fashion *nightmare.*

"Gold leaf? Baubles? The WBC belt is a fashion-backward mélange of last season's styles. As an accessory, it's about as appropriate for a heavyweight champ as a Hello Kitty purse.

"And where have I seen that color scheme before?" Valcarcel continued, his tone growing ever more sarcastic. "Was it on my grandmother's shower curtains, or Hef's Grotto in '74? Puh-*leeze.*

"The last WBO bout was billed as 'The Clash on Sunset Strip,'" Valcarcel concluded, rolling his eyes. "But a more accurate name would be 'The Clash of Grotesque Pastels.'"

© John Gurzinski/AFP/Getty Images

Ripken!
Wilkins! McEnroe!

The Biggest Names in Sports Will Be There—
Set your DVR now.

ESPN2 presents a once-in-a-lifetime collection of America's most impressive athletes, together for the first time at the ESPY2 Awards.

The evening will feature Baltimore Orioles legend Billy Ripken, two-time NBA Slam Dunk contestant Gerald Wilkins, and '80s tennis champ and broadcaster Patrick McEnroe, all under one roof.

Who will win the coveted Vince DiMaggio silver statuette? Join us Sunday night, March 10, at 7 P.M. Mountain to find out.

This unforgettable event will be hosted by Greg Gumbel and broadcast live from the James Franklin Center in downtown Philadelphia. Joining Gumbel will be a star-studded lineup of America's hottest performers, including recording artist Ashlee Simpson and a special appearance by the world-renowned "Man from Hope," Roger Clinton.

And for those who live near the City of Brotherly Love, come on down! Famed bad-boy author Ozzie Canseco will also be on hand, giving away and signing advance copies of his soon-to-be-finished exposé of minor league baseball.

Also—you thrilled to his exploits in college, now you can meet one of football's most electrifying space-based vehicles: The Missile, Qadry Ismail.

Proceeds benefit the Daffy Dean Foundation.

A Walk's As Good As A Hit

BY JEFF COLVIN

Come on, Teddy, you can do it!

A walk's as good as a hit.

Good eye now, Teddy, good eye. Don't swing at the bad ones.

That's ball one. Way to go, you're a quarter of the way there!

Whoa, that one was over your head, Teddy. Try to lay off those. We need you on base, sport.

Choke up a bit.

Great eye! Way to lay off the wild pitch. Two and one, kid, two and one. You're halfway to victory. Hang tough, Teddy. Don't swing unless it's perfect.

GREAT cut! Way to swing for the fences. But again: Try not to swing if it's over your head.

Okay, two strikes now. Gotta protect the plate.

Way to make contact! I knew you could do it. A foul ball is a great step in the right direction.

All right, hang tough. Another foul would really send the message that you're in it to win it.

Atta boy! Way to get a piece of it! Two straight fouls—you're on fire now, champ.

Choke up more.

Okay, it's gonna be tough to pull it off now, Teddy—this guy is really throwing well.

Hey, remember that time you almost reached first base on a dropped third strike? Maybe you can do that again!

Remember: If you believe in yourself, you can do anything!

Jeff is Teddy's coach

A Walk's As Good As A Hit-By-Pitch

BY IRV SNYDER

Come on, Teddy, you probably can't do it.

Contrary to the old adage, a walk is not as good as a hit. A walk is, in fact, precisely as good as a hit-by-pitch.

And barring a miracle, Teddy, a walk and a hit-by-pitch are just about the only two options you've got.

All right, good eye now, Teddy, good eye. Try to get plunked by the bad ones.

That's ball one. Way to go, you've never been ahead in the count before.

That was the worst swing I've ever seen. Do us a favor and don't swing at the next pitch, okay? Thank you.

Two and one, Teddy. You're halfway to becoming an instant hidden-ball-trick victim.

Okay, scratch what I said about your last swing—it's now the *second*-worst swing I've ever seen.

Two strikes now, Teddy. Say your prayers.

Way to make contact—I didn't think you had it in you. A foul ball is a strike.

All right, hang tough. Another foul ball would make this one of the best at-bats of your career.

Two straight fouls. I'm calling the school paper.

Choke up more.

Okay, it's gonna be tough to pull it off now, Teddy—this guy is really throwing well, and your only hit of the season was when you accidentally laid down a perfect bunt.

Remember: If you believe in yourself, you're nuts.

Irv is Teddy's father

NASCAR Rookie Asked To Stop Using Turn Signals

Veterans irked by frequent beeping of horn, eating in car

Robert LaBerge/Getty Images Sport/Getty Images

F ollowing his fourth-place finish in the Auto Club 500, veteran racers have asked first-year driver J. D. Spickle to stop flouting NASCAR tradition by leaving his blinker on during races.

"If he wants to carry the extra weight, that's his problem," said Kurt Busch, "but technically, he shouldn't even have taillights."

"It's one thing to politely let us know when you're pullin' out of the pit," said Matt Kenseth. "But to leave that damn thing blinking for 123 laps? Hey, buddy, I know you're making a left turn. Those are all we do out here."

This is not the first time Spickle has drawn the ire of race opponents. He has been warned by race officials for flashing his high beams at Dale Earnhardt Jr. and for having the interior of his blue no. 72 Chevy

> ## "It's one thing to politely let us know when you're pullin' out of the pit. But to leave that damn thing blinking for 123 laps? Hey, buddy, I know you're making a left turn. Those are all we do out here."

vacuumed during pit stops.

Says Jeff Gordon, "I'm all for safety, but when there's a caution flag out after a wreck, you don't have to put on your hazards, for cryin' out loud. I also don't know why he has to pull out his cell phone every time there's a crash and act like he's frantically dialing highway patrol."

Reached at home while taking an online driver education course, Spickle seemed nonplussed by the charges.

"Look, I flashed Dale because I wanted to pass the guy. It's the proper thing to do. That's how my mama raised me. Those guys racin' around like that without turn lamps, they should stick an arm out the window and use hand signals. It's not just common sense—it's the law.

"As for the other stuff: I don't like dirty air, and I don't like a dirty car. Sometimes I spill my soda. Nobody got mad when Richard Petty broke out the Armor All. What's the big deal if I like to change the air freshener every couple hundred miles? I'm in that thing all gosh darn day."

Despite a penchant for pit-stopping to adjust his subwoofer and empty his ashtray, Spickle is ranked no. 55 in Nextel Cup standings. ∎

Steroids? STEROIDS?

BY J. B. GALISHAW

Unbelievable. Just unbelievable. And I thought I knew professional athletes. Thuggish violence? Sure. Sexual assault? Of course. But steroids?! C'mon fellas, that stuff's bad for you! Your bodies are your livelihoods!

I mean, when you punch the crap out of someone half your size, or force yourself on some frail 19-year-old sliver of a girl, I totally understand: You're not risking your own safety, so why the hell not?

If there's one thing I thought I could count on from professional athletes, it's that their unhealthy aggression would always be directed outwardly. But self-abuse—that's not for winners!

> ## If there's one thing I thought I could count on from professional athletes, it's that their unhealthy aggression would always be directed outwardly. But self-abuse—that's not for winners!

When the Kobe Bryant story broke, it was easy for me to explain to my 9-year-old son why an athlete might rape a woman—because humans are

inherently selfish, with dark uncontrollable urges to hurt others—but how can I look him in the eye and explain that his favorite player would actually do harm *to his own person?* I might as well tell him there's no Easter Bunny.

Frankly, I'm still inclined to give these guys the benefit of the doubt. Barry Bonds said he thought the steroids he used were flaxseed oil, and I believe him. Flaxseed oil promotes healthy skin, hair, and nails; steroids inflate you like a balloon, send you into fits of rage, and shrink your testicles to the size of capers. So it's pretty easy to understand the mix-up.

And all Jason Giambi admitted to was "testosterone"—hey, if that's a crime, then never mind the players, you could probably suspend 90 percent of the fans. Hell, I've wanted to fondle every women's tennis player I've laid eyes on since I was 12. Should I be banned from the U.S. Open?

There is a sacred trust between athletes and their fans, and it is in grave danger of being broken these days. I just hope that this whole mess can be cleared up soon, and that we can once again be comfortable in the knowledge that if pro athletes are doing permanent, unspeakable bodily harm to someone, it's not themselves. ■

J. B. Galishaw is our senior editor and the editor of The Kournikova Reader.

Our recurring feature in which we revisit the sports lore of simpler times, via the *SMTM* archives

Latest Congressional Hearings Address Instant Replay, Flat Ball-park Beer, Other National Concerns

After the 11-hour hearings on steroids in baseball, this week Congress continued to tackle a wide range of urgent domestic issues.

Mr. Selig, the statistics are startling: In 1985 only 30,000 high school students had tried it. Today the number is close to half a million. Kids emulate what they see in the Major Leagues, and if you continue to let this cancer afflict your sport, then before you know it little leaguers will be succumbing.

Abolish the designated hitter rule, or Congress will do it for you.
—*Sen. Jim Bunning (R-Ky.)*

"Body armor?" Is that what this is about? Some sort of psychic body armor? Tell that to our troops in Iraq, who desperately need the real stuff right now. Skin art has no place in basketball.
—*Rep. Chris Shays (R-Conn.), Chairman, Senate Task Force on Tattoos*

My problem with instant replay is primarily the time spent in limbo. Did the receiver have possession of the ball? Was there defensive interference on the play? Valuable minutes are ticking away. We need an efficient solution. That's why my

colleagues and I have prepared this 216-page report on the subject. I'm told the executive branch seeks involvement here as well.
—*Rep. Elijah Cummings (D-Md.)*

I have not been reassured one bit by the testimony I have heard today. Not one bit. This is a moral outrage. We cannot sit idly by as our nation slouches toward Gomorrah on the wings of the Arizona Cardinals.
—*Rep. Stephen F. Lynch (D-Mass.), addressing the recent trend of lackluster Monday Night Football matchups*

We have a war going on, gentlemen, and it's between a communal sense of decency and your garish jerseys.
—*Rep. Henry Waxman (D-Calif.) addressing assembled members of the Kansas State Wildcats during the two-day Team Uniforms hearings*

I'm not sure I can describe it definitively, but, like Justice Potter Stewart's description of pornography, I know it when I see it.
—*Umpire John Hirschbeck, explaining baseball's balk rule during the House's emergency session of March 25*

You know, a lot of us on this committee care so very deeply about the game of basketball. I grew up in the town of Morris, Indiana. Population 1,200. Roundball is pretty much religion where I come from. I would practice my jump shot from dawn 'til dusk on those endless summer days. To me, and millions like me, basketball is much, much more than a game. It's a way of life. So why don't you call traveling anymore?
—*Rep. Mark Edward Souder (R-Ind.) to NBA officials*

THIS MONTH IN HISTORY

March 2, 1953
House Un-American Activities Committee orders Grange, Holzman, Smith, and Barber to add "White And Blue" to first names.

March 6–13, 1987
Christo wraps Manute Bol in green Kevlar for Bullets homestand.

VOLUME 100, NO. 5

APRIL

SPORTS MAGAZINE

THE MAGAZINE

March Madness Rolls On:
U.S. Continuing Cinderella Story

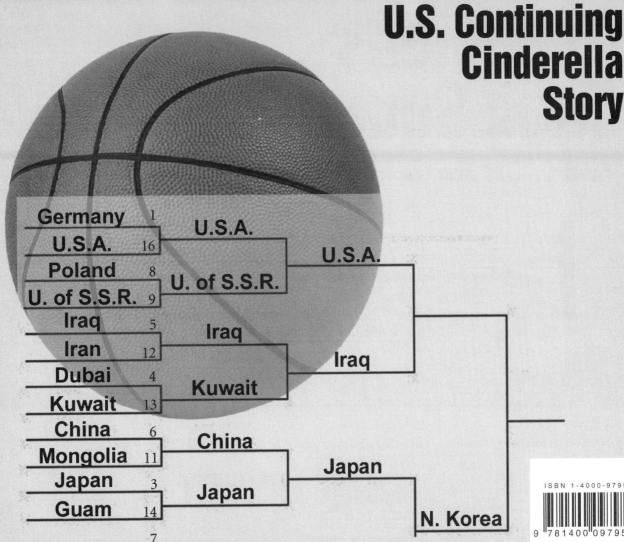

Germany	1			
U.S.A.	16	U.S.A.		
Poland	8		U.S.A.	
U. of S.S.R.	9	U. of S.S.R.		
Iraq	5			
Iran	12	Iraq		
Dubai	4		Iraq	
Kuwait	13	Kuwait		
China	6			
Mongolia	11	China		
Japan	3		Japan	
Guam	14	Japan		
	7			N. Korea

ISBN 1-4000-9795-9

9 781400 097951

Upstart Nation Wearing Down Tenacious Arab Squad

Original field soon narrowed to Final Four

The glass slipper, it seems, still fits the young republic. The United States has continued its unlikely advance, building a commanding advantage over a more established Mesopotamian foe.

Despite facing opponents with far greater tournament experience, the United States has made a big splash since arriving on the scene in just 1776. Like Gonzaga, America is the kind of plucky underdog people love to pick in their office pools.

"Although no one knew much about them at the time," explains David Katz, editor of *College Basketball Insider,* "the Americans were building confidence with that preseason wipe-out of the Indians. That was just a massacre. And in an away game, too."

Fans first took note of the fledgling squad after early victories over the British (twice), and Mexico.

"Even though they barely had an offense back then," said bank manager Aaron Furman, studying a printout of his tournament picks, "you knew these guys could make some noise come tourney time."

The Americans endured a midseason lull, including a team scuffle during the 1860s that divided the locker room for nearly five years. Unity thrived again under head coach Teddy Roosevelt, and the Americans resumed their attack with renewed vigor, pounding out easy victories over lesser, nonconference foes like Spain and Panama.

"They scheduled a lot of patsies to pad their record," noted Katz, "which led to their almost not getting a dance card."

Like Gonzaga, America is the kind of plucky underdog people love to pick in their office pools.

A late addition to the championship tournament, the Yanks scored big early-round victories over Germany and Japan.

"That's as far as I had them going," said Furman, furrowing his brow. "But then in the Sweet Sixteen they really came up big against the U. of S.S.R."

Under brash head coach George W. Bush, the United States has been more aggressive on offense than ever. Bush and assistant coach Donald Rumsfeld stress a "run-and-shoot" strategy on the court and incendiary trash-talking off it, drawing the ire of veteran coaches like Jacques Chirac.

Despite being loudly jeered in most arenas, the United States finds itself on the verge of the Final Four. "If they win this, their next game's gonna be a tough one," mused Katz. "North Korea has a lot of weapons." ■

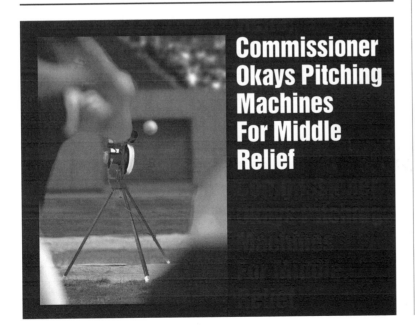

Commissioner Okays Pitching Machines For Middle Relief

Woeful Season Blamed On "Liberal Media"

In a 30-minute tirade following his team's seventh consecutive loss, a 96–91 defeat to the Indiana Pacers on February 15, Denver Nuggets assistant coach Ashton Parker attributed his squad's 14–27 record to "journalistic bias."

"I'm sick and tired of liberal taste-makers in the media elite anointing 'winners' and 'losers' according to the left-wing agenda of their editorial boards," said Coach Parker. "Do you have any idea how difficult it is for us to play so doggone hard, leave it all out there on the basketball court, then wake up the next day to headlines that scream we lost the game by five points?

"It's one thing to allege we committed 23 turnovers against the Warriors in a credible publication, but when the *San Francisco Chronicle*—which takes its marching orders from Michael Moore and Al Franken—writes that, I say consider the source.

"So the wine-sippers at the *New York Times* say we haven't won a game in two weeks? How is that the 'paper of record'? Um, Jayson Blair anyone?"

Told that the *Times'* claim was in fact correct, Coach Parker remarked, "Listen. The *L.A. Times* lists us in fifth place. This from a paper that endorsed Michael Dukakis!

"Every time I see a headline in one of those Volvo-mom rags like the *Washington Post,* it's always negative: Pacers Lose. Pacers Win Breaks Long Losing Streak. How about, Pacers Win Launches Possible Winning Streak?

> ## "The Red Sox—the darling of the loony left— have never faced this kind of negativity from the Brie-eating Boston sports media."

"It's one thing to provide an objective account, quite another to give a statistical breakdown of our rebounding deficiencies in a four-color exploded graph in *USA Today.* I thought they taught ethics at J-school?

"It's just not fair. The Red Sox—the darling of the loony left—have never faced this kind of negativity from the Brie-eating Boston sports media. You guys, most of you guys really have it in for teams like mine, who work hard, play by the rules, and represent heartland values."

Informed by reporter Richard Altman that his team was called for 28 infractions during the game, including 19 fouls, Coach Parker challenged his credentials.

"Please, Rich, aren't you from CNN? Folks—find me a hack without a socialist agenda to ask the question, and I'll answer it.

"Today's *Seattle Post-Intelligencer* says that we've lost the most home games in the conference. I beg of you, NBA beat reporters, leave the America-hating to Hollywood and Harvard.

"And TNT, it's almost like having Al Jazeera broadcasting NBA games. When you have Jane Fonda's ex-husband in charge, you get analysts like Kenny Smith saying our frontcourt doesn't rotate the ball enough. I've got news for you, Mr. Latte-Loving Minority Journalist: Call 'em how you see 'em, not how the ACLU does.

"Look—I'm sure Hillary Clinton thinks I should have gone to the bench earlier against Dallas, but I can't be bothered with that stuff. We're trying to win a playoff berth here, not conform to some NPR-listener's idea of what a winning basketball team should be.

"When I want to see how America thinks we're doing, I check out the *Wall St. Journal*. They don't have a sports section." ■

OVERHEARD

Our correspondents keep their ears open and their recording devices on

The following was observed at a recent NBA game.

One Game Not Taken At A Time

Listen, coach. I'm out there, I see the screen coming, I see the open man, but then I'm thinking about three weeks from now when we play the Nuggets. They're gonna trap us all day!

So we gotta spread the floor. Also, tonight, looks like number eleven has a weak left hand. So let's overplay his right, and when we play New York next Monday, sub in Bobby on D to go against their big forwards.

Same thing with the Rockets. What are we, down five? Late second period? Jeez. I need 35 tickets for the Charlotte game, I got family down there. How about we try a pick and roll off the inbounds? Hey, who plays center for the Hawks?

They're zoning us, I know. That's why I'm trying to post up number twenty-five. He reminds me of that guy on the Bulls, came from the CBA two years ago? Let me bring the ball up court next time. It's like I keep saying: We win five of our next seven and beat the Mavs at home like we should, we're in the driver's seat come playoff time and on that last play Derrick was open underneath.

Crime Rampant Among NBA Mascots

Commissioner denounces league's "cuddliest thugs"

NBA commissioner David Stern held a press conference last month to address the recent rash of criminal acts by NBA mascots.

"The NBA can no longer tolerate such behavior from the league's most visible members—whether it be the superstar shooting guard accused of rape, or the guy in the purple moose costume charged with brutally beating a ballboy during a halftime heroin transaction."

Stern's press conference was precipitated by disturbing reports from Los Angeles charging "C.C. The Clipper Coyote," who is eight feet tall and orange, with groping a female league employee while "visibly drunk, bloated, and in costume."

"This is a very upsetting story, but hardly a unique one," said Stern, noting that this was the sixth criminal incident this season among the league's mascots, and the fourth involving groping.

"Every member of the NBA family must fully understand the responsibility that comes with putting on a uniform," Stern said, "whether that uniform says 'Pistons' or 'Lakers' or is simply a big, fluffy hybrid of an octopus and a circus clown with the number zero on front."

The NBA is far from alone. According to experts, mascot misbehavior is a widespread phenomenon in pro, college, and even recreational leagues. Ruby Nissen, author of *Not So Cute on the*

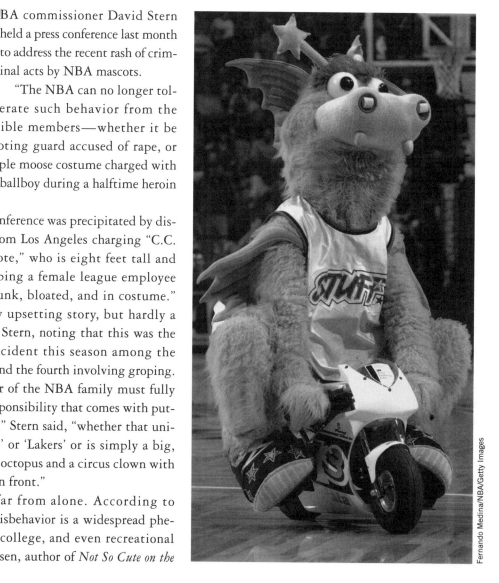

Fernando Medina/NBA/Getty Images

The lovable Denver Nuggets Thingamajig was found guilty on three counts of asexual assault.

Inside, the hefty 2002 book exploring mascot psychology, attributes mascot delinquency to an identity crisis:

"A lot of these costumes are so abstract, people can't even tell what they're supposed to be. I think we've all been at a game and had this reaction: 'Okay, it's big and it's green . . . but otherwise, I got nothing. Is it from the sea? Or outer space? Or maybe it's a dinosaur? And regardless—why is it jumping on a trampoline?' For the fans, that's merely a confusing diversion during a timeout. But for the person sweltering inside, it can be an ongoing psychodrama."

Journeyman mascot Edwin Ramishwar agrees: "It's not as if team management or anyone knows what some of these things are. NOBODY does. Sure, if the team name is the Bears or the Sharks, then it's usually clear. But what if the team is called the Hurricanes or the Browns or the 76ers? Then you're pretty much left guessing."

"And believe me," he added, "it's not easy to perform for 15,000 people if, after three years on the job, you still have to ask yourself, right before show time, 'Do I or do I not have a penis?' "

The potential consequences of such identity crises became painfully clear in January, when the lovable Denver Nuggets Thingamajig was found guilty on three counts of asexual assault.

Ted Giannoulas, better known as the San Diego Chicken, feels that the mascot's moment may have passed: "I'd hate to be starting out in the business today: a million mascots, none that anyone can name. When I debuted, in 1974, I was the first and only mascot around. And it wasn't exactly a challenge to figure out what I was supposed to be.

"I think I was just in the right place at the right time. After Vietnam, and Watergate, the country was ready for something uplifting. Like a big chicken. It just struck a chord." ∎

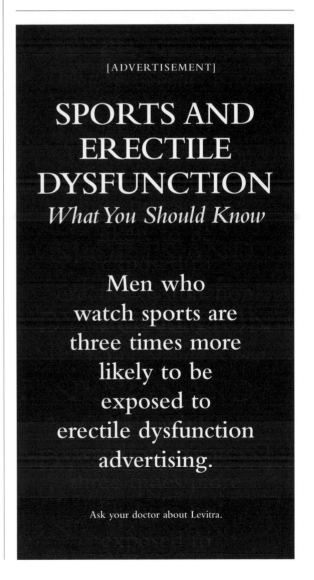

We scour the Web so you don't have to

The following is taken from talkingbaseballtoday.com, our pick for best online hot stove discussion.

Baseball Message Board

MARCH 25, 3:43 P.M. EST

Schilling62: I totally disagree with Schilling29 about Schilling—he'll be fine, he's a gamer. Schilling273 was right.

PumpsieGreen: Agree—Schill will pitch at least 2 more years, maybe 3. Wants to get into Hall of Fame. Many milestones in sight. 200 wins, 3000 Ks, etc.

nukelaloosh: already deserves hall one of best postseason pitchers ever case closed. who was a better player tommy john or deion sanders? i say deion b/c better all round athlete.

90feet: Sorry Nuke, but postseason performance has never been guarantee of Hall. Check the record books, Schill's only had 7 great seasons in his career—needs 2 or 3 more to get into Hall.

MendozaLine: Says who? Koufax only had 6 great seasons.

90feet: Those weren't just "great" seasons, they were legendary. They include 3 of the 7 greatest pitching seasons of all time (Pedro '99/'00, Gibson '68, Walter Johnson '13). Schilling doesn't have one season in the top 46. Also: is anyone else outraged that innocent animals are slaughtered to make baseballs?

mesabath: agree deion better than TJ. speed kills. longevity overrated.

nukelaloosh: yeah boy. which was better '75 world series or last episode of friends? i say friends b/c better ending.

MendozaLine: Schill's stats look less impressive than Koufax's b/c Schill pitches in high-scoring era, Koufax pitched in low-scoring era. Schill belongs in Hall.

90feet: PLEASE! Koufax threw 4 no-hitters in a 4 year span. How many no-hitters has your boyfriend Curt Schilling thrown? What was that? A little louder? Zero? THAT'S WHAT I THOUGHT!

FreddyBallgame: Agree, Friends finale better than '75 series. '75 series great but inconsistent: Games 1 and 5 total yawners. BUT Game 6 taken on its own WAY better than last Friends, better than '91 game 7, almost as good as last M*A*S*H.

MendozaLine: Since when did no-hitters matter for the Hall?! Johnny Vander Meer threw back to back no-hitters, should we put him in Cooperstown? Oh no, I guess not—considering his career record was 119–121. GET A CLUE, 90feet. Re your other question: yes, very disturbed by the slaughtered animals.

RoyalsFan: Just saw one of the greatest plays I've ever seen. 4th inning, Royals/Pirates split-squad, second to last game of spring training. Ball hit to the gap, Chip Ambres going full speed, sees he can't get a glove on it, so he sticks his leg out, total hockey move, total kick-save. Prevents ball from going to the wall, saves at least one run, maybe two. KC lost

10–2 but just seeing that play gave me really high hopes for this year.

90feet: I WASN'T JUST TALKING ABOUT THE NO-HITTERS! FORGET THE NO-HITTERS! SCHILLING ISN'T IN KOUFAX'S LEAGUE. HE COULDN'T HOLD KOUFAX'S JOCK.

MendozaLine: SCHILLING ALREADY HAS MORE CAREER WINS THAN KOUFAX! AND HE'S STILL PITCHING!! HOW DO YOU EXPLAIN THAT ONE?!

90feet: KOUFAX HAD TO RETIRE AT AGE 30 BECAUSE OF ARM INJURIES! HE WOULD HAVE WON 300 IF HE HAD STAYED HEALTHY!!

MendozaLine: COULDA SHOULDA WOULDA!! Also, I've heard that scientists in Europe are experimenting with a rubberized ball—could be the solution to the equine genocide.

Killebrew: Greetings. Excellent site, great discussions. Question: since when are there THREE divisions in each league?

Fernandomania22: hey guys what's up, had to go out of town for a funeral, trying to catch up on 3 days of discussion so here goes . . . agree with RazorShines63 that d-backs should trade shawn green for minor league pitching prospects, disagree with KellyLeak38 that seattle should try to deal joel pineiro for a lefty power hitter, agree with JohnnyDickshot136 about the blue jays pitching staff but not about kurosawa's later films, agree with Spaceman75 about banning DH, legalizing THC, agree with nukelaloosh that '98 yanks were better than '82 islanders but not as good as sugar ray robinson, COMPLETELY disagree that 2001 world series was better than led zep 4. slaughter of horses to make baseballs very troubling. ∎

Baseball's Greatest Numbers

56—Tip dollars left by Joe DiMaggio, career

.406—Percentage of Ted Williams available for purchase

61—Times Roger Maris's single-season home-run record has been broken since 1998

1.12—Bob Gibson, career smiles

4,192—Times Pete Rose denied betting on baseball, before confessing

Q&A: Dick Vitale

Dick Vitale, one of the country's premier college basketball analysts, took time out from his busy schedule to answer questions from our readers.

Q Dick, I got a question. I'm a big Florida Gators fan. What did you think of Eminem's third album, *The Eminem Show?*
—*Darrin, Sarasota, Fla.*

A Oh, I thought it was another BIG-TIME performance, Darrin. He really came through. With Em, it's all about one thing: INTENSITY, baby! You just know you're gonna get 110 percent.

And HOW does he stay ahead of the competition? Well, just like all PTPers, he'll keep ya GUESSIN', baby!

One minute he's gettin' all reflective, doin' "Sing for the Moment" with Aerosmith, then the next minute he's got his 5-year-old daughter on the mic, shriekin', "My Dad's Gone Crazy!" Just UNBELIEVABLE, baby! There is NO WAY to defend against that!

Q Mr. Vitale, what is your favorite food?
—*Marcy, Champaign, Ill.*

A Wow, such a tough question, Marcy. So hard to choose just ONE, baby!

I think when it's all said and done, I go with CARROTS. They got all kindsa vitamins, nutrients . . . For cryin' out loud, Marcy, they even improve your EYESIGHT! There's just NO OTHER VEGETABLE in the game that can really say that!

And let me tell ya somethin' about carrots: They're so VERSATILE! Talk about playin' all five

positions on the floor! They're great raw, cooked . . . It just doesn't matter! And you can make 'em into absolutely ANYTHING, Marcy! A soup, a juice . . . even a cake, baby! A CAKE!

Q Hey, Dick, you're the man. Jayhawks rock!! What's your favorite movie?
—*Phil, Lawrence, Kan.*

A Oh Philly baby, you're talkin' my language! I'm a film nut, Phil. A flat-out nut. But it's just like my buddy Marcy askin' about my favorite food—how can I choose just one?

Well let me run through a few off the top of my head. Ya got *Rocky*—the ultimate underdog, a story that never gets old. And bein' a hoops guy, how could I fail to mention *Hoosiers?* The greatest basketball movie ever, no question about it! And then there's *Mon Oncle,* Jacques Tati's visually stunning satire of contemporary mores.

But when it comes to my absolute, all-time number one, I gotta go with the achingly tender *Fried Green Tomatoes.* SO MUCH HUMANITY, BABY!

Around the same time this movie came out, the University of Michigan basketball squad had a starting lineup that people were calling the Fab Five. That's all well and good, but if you ask me, let's talk about the Fab Four: Idgie, Ruth, Evelyn, and Ninny! That's a lineup that was built to win!

Q Dick, what's the craziest thing a woman's ever done with you in bed?
—*Jeff, Vacaville, Calif.*

When it comes to my absolute, all-time number one, I gotta go with the achingly tender *Fried Green Tomatoes*. SO MUCH HUMANITY, BABY!

Whoa, Jeff, let's not get carried away, baby! There are certain things that I just can't get into. Not here anyway!

That being said, I'd have to go back to my college days. I met a girl at a party—she was cute as a button, Jeff, but I could see in her eyes that she was WILD. Anyway, later on in my dorm room, one thing leads to another, and she's—how should I put this?—PLEASURIN' ME, BABY! So far so good, right, Jeff? But then, before I know it, I feel somethin' I'll never, ever forget, just as memorable as NC State '83—this girl is gettin' all GNASHY with her TEETH!

Thank God I had a timeout remaining, Jeff, because I called it RIGHT THEN AND THERE! ∎

LOST & FOUND

Our correspondents are always on the lookout for noteworthy sports artifacts

The following was found in the bleacher seats at a San Francisco Giants game.

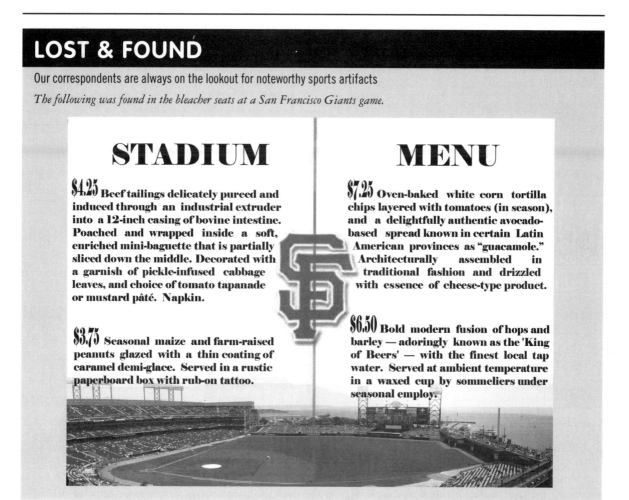

STADIUM

$4.25 Beef tailings delicately pureed and induced through an industrial extruder into a 12-inch casing of bovine intestine. Poached and wrapped inside a soft, enriched mini-baguette that is partially sliced down the middle. Decorated with a garnish of pickle-infused cabbage leaves, and choice of tomato tapanade or mustard pâté. Napkin.

$3.75 Seasonal maize and farm-raised peanuts glazed with a thin coating of caramel demi-glace. Served in a rustic paperboard box with rub-on tattoo.

MENU

$7.25 Oven-baked white corn tortilla chips layered with tomatoes (in season), and a delightfully authentic avocado-based spread known in certain Latin American provinces as "guacamole." Architecturally assembled in traditional fashion and drizzled with essence of cheese-type product.

$6.50 Bold modern fusion of hops and barley — adoringly known as the 'King of Beers' — with the finest local tap water. Served at ambient temperature in a waxed cup by sommeliers under seasonal employ.

Rave Reviews For Tell-Some Book

U ntil last month, even the most diehard baseball fan could not claim to know much, if anything, about former Major League pitcher Tyler Cayton (Milwaukee 1986, Milwaukee / Cleveland / Detroit/Milwaukee '87, Toledo Mud Hens '88, Yomiuri Giants '89–'93).

Yet in the four weeks since the release of his memoir *Right Down the Middle,* Cayton has been the talk of the sports world. Fans and critics numbed by years of sensationalistic "tell-alls" are responding with enthusiasm to Cayton's some-holds-barred account of life in the big leagues. The shortage of shocking, back-stabbing, unsubstantiated accusations is more than made up for by Cayton's warmth, gentle humor, and gift for the flinching anecdote. Excerpts:

CHAPTER 5

By now most everyone knows about amphetamines, or "greenies," and it's true: Baseball players pop 'em like M&M's. But what we really popped like M&M's, were M&M's.

When I was on the Brewers, I played with a couple of future Hall of Famers by the names of Paul Molitor and Robin Yount. Well, the two of them had developed this game to kill time—on plane rides, in hotels, and such—where you pick an M&M out of the bag, without looking, and if it's brown it's an out, yellow a single, orange a double, and so on. Green was a home run, so we'd always call a homer

> ## The shortage of shocking, back-stabbing, unsubstantiated accusations is more than made up for . . .

a "greenie" and have a big laugh about it.

For a while we used to chase each "greenie" with a shot of whiskey. But we didn't have the stomach to keep that up for very long, so pretty soon we switched to Coca-Cola.

CHAPTER 6

. . . Steroids were rampant in the league. Each team had at least a few users. I still remember to this day: In the break between games of a doubleheader against Texas, I walked into the clubhouse, and guess who I saw using steroids? No really, guess.

CHAPTER 7

Athletes on the road are like wild animals. No morals, no conscience, no recollection of a wife back home. They'll screw anything that moves. One time in Anaheim, when two of the guys on the team, both married, were at a brothel getting intimately acquainted with two transvestite hookers, me, Ehnert, Bodine, and DeLuca snuck onto the local mini-golf course and played a delirious nine holes under the midnight moonlight. ∎

Our recurring feature in which we revisit the sports lore of simpler times, via the *SMTM* archives

Homophobic Remarks Somehow No Big Deal

Apparently the nation has not been shocked, jolted, or even mildly stirred by antigay remarks voiced in late March by Colorado Rockies pitcher Todd Jones.

Despite declaring, "I wouldn't want a gay guy being around me . . . Yeah, he's got rights or whatever, but he shouldn't walk around proud. It's like he's rubbing it in our face," Jones has not enjoyed the same media fanfare as others before him.

Explained radio host Don Imus, "*Nightline,* Leno, CNN—they were all over John Rocker, but they're not touching this. And who can blame them? I'm falling asleep reading these remarks. What Rocker said was so vivid, so gripping. His line about New York being filled with 'Asians and Koreans' and 'Spanish people'? Great stuff. But this dude is so bland. He didn't even bother to throw in any epithets. He must have had a really bad PR guy."

NBC anchor Tom Brokaw, who covered the Rocker story in 1999 and conducted a lengthy Internet search to find the Jones story, agreed: "Rocker's remarks really caught on. People everywhere could relate, whether they hated 'kids with purple hair,' '20-year-old moms with four kids,' or just 'queers with AIDS.' He had that common touch. But Jones was so discriminatory in his discrimination. These days, it's all about *inclusiveness.*"

The gay community was hardly surprised by Jones's comments. "This is professional sports, so we've come to expect it," said David Tumanov of the Gay & Lesbian Alliance Against Defamation. "Judging from his remarks, Jones seems to think the first openly gay player is gonna act like Liberace. And then

Rockies' Pitcher To Gays: Hear Me Roar

there's the team's nonapology apology, in which the Rockies affirm that they support all people, 'regardless of race, color, sex, religion, national orientation, age, disability, or status as a veteran.' Well that sure covers everything . . . except sexuality! 'Status as a veteran'? Yeah, that's a real concern in pro sports—all the veteran-bashing." ∎

THIS MONTH IN HISTORY

April 24, 1987
Oh to Be Oddibe McDowell, Bart Giamatti's iambic tribute to baseball's marginal talents, tops *New York Times* bestseller list.

April 16, 1990
First African American owner of fantasy team.

VOLUME 100, NO. 6

MAY

SPORTS MAGAZINE

THE MAGAZINE

BASEBALL INSTITUTES SALARY CAPS

ISBN 1-4000-9795-9

9 781400 097951

Baseball Debuts Salary Caps

This season Major League Baseball has begun official use of salary caps. In place of traditional team headgear, players now don ball caps displaying the wearer's annual pretax earnings. According to MLB officials, the new look will make the game more relevant to today's fans.

"Gone are the tired team logos of yesteryear," said MLB spokesperson Nancy Coplan, wearing a size 7 purple $155,000 salary cap. "An oriole? A grinning Indian? You got to be kidding. This is the 21st century. And besides, the way players jump around these days, team affiliation is passé. Salary caps are a concept any American can support."

According to MLB officials, the new look will make the game more relevant to today's fans.

Tugging at the bill of his blue and white $8,500,000 cap, Cubs fireballer Kerry Wood remarked, "I don't understand why the union was against this. It's comfy, fits great, and lets everyone know the score. I love it!"

Said Astros manager Phil Garner, "From a strategy standpoint, it's a godsend. Say you've got a 10-mill-per guy up against a reliever earning mid-six-figures. Right away you know you've got a mismatch."

As expected, fans seemed to have taken to the new caps immediately. "Now if a guy flubs an easy grounder," remarked one bleacher denizen in Pittsburgh, "I can yell, 'three-point-four mill for that?' It's a more exact heckle."

Coplan explained that player salary caps are not available for purchase, but for $19.95 fans can secure their own personalized model. "All you need to do," Coplan said, "is walk into any store selling officially licensed MLB apparel and provide a copy of your most recent W-2." ■

Historic 2,000th Ascent Lauded at Mount Everest Summit Kinko's

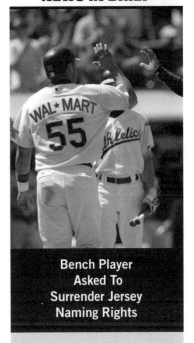

MLB: Pitchers Allowed To Ice Arm Between Batters

Average game approaching six hours

Despite efforts to quicken the already glacial pace of Major League games, a little-known clause in the baseball rule book has extended the game beyond all previous dimensions.

Rule 8.04(B), instituted in 1890 by factory-team owners looking to keep their employees healthy for industrial work, allows pitchers to take "all necessary steps" to avoid injury while pitching. Although it had never been previously invoked, this year several hurlers are exploiting the rule.

"It's in the book, so it's legal," says Rockies starter Jason Knudson, a leading proponent of on-field icing. Knudson often piles three ice packs and a sling on the mound, next to the rosin bag. "I don't always do it, but sometimes my shoulder gets tight, or I feel a little soreness coming on while working through the heart of the order, so I slap on a chill bag and let it sit for a while."

> " … they get upset when the trainer comes out with my warm-up jacket, tube of liniment, and MP3 player."

"It keeps me fresh," said Mariners rookie reliever Ryan Eddy, known for performing on-mound yoga. "Especially with a full count."

As between-pitch icing delays and deltoid massages have lasted up to 25 minutes, fans in the stands have grown weary.

"We used to give away bobble-heads and trading cards," says Texas Rangers director of promotions Len Ginsberg, "but we got so many requests for pillows that we started giving those away instead." This summer, stadium vendors have sold a record number of team logo eyeshades. Yet some fans have shaken off the onset of slumber to voice their displeasure at the interminable delays.

"Look, fans boo when I throw over to first," said Eddy. "So I'm not surprised they get upset when the trainer comes out with my warm-up jacket, tube of liniment, and MP3 player."

"Fans shouldn't whine," says Blue Jays veteran Rich De La Fuente, who spent 15 minutes stretching his rotator cuff in the third inning of a scoreless tie last week. "This is my livelihood. It's not like I'm going full R-I-C-E—Rest, Ice, Compression, Elevation—after every pitch, which is what I *should* do. I only do it when I feel a twinge, and I've got a runner on third."

Batters have also complained about the often indeterminate waits between pitches, to no avail. Changes to the rulebook are not permitted under the current labor agreement.

"Have you ever really read this thing?" asks Astros pitching coach Marv Brown, holding up a dog-eared copy of the *Official Major League Baseball Rule Book.* "Turns out, if a pitcher doesn't like the feel of a certain baseball, he can request a smoke break." ∎

Street-Baller Yearns For Fundamentals, Yesteryear

Star swingman Allen "Jam-Z" Watkins, of the Junction Boulevard courts across from Wendy's in Queens, N.Y., revealed that he merely pretends to enjoy trash-talking and showmanship while privately longing for a return to basketball fundamentals.

Jam-Z succumbing to peer pressure

After begrudgingly showcasing his between-the-legs dribble, gratuitous crossover move, and Jordan-style tongue-wag throughout a 21–15 victory in a pickup game, Watkins waxed romantic about "sensible, team-oriented basketball."

"To be frank, the current variety of flashy, 'look-at-me' hoops is just silly. And a little sad. How insecure must one be to engage in such endless one-upmanship? Where is the roundball of old—the well-executed screen, the two-handed set-shot, the no-no-look pass?

"Each time I dunk on a guy and then stand over him saying that was nothing compared to what I did to his mother . . . well, I die a little."

Watkins then entered a new game, where he promptly executed a thunderous two-handed tomahawk jam. He proceeded to swagger up and down the court throughout, shouting, "How's that taste? Huh?? Who's your daddy? QUIEN ES TU PAPA?!"

Yet, his eyes—moist and a bit distant—said, "Nice game."

Athletes Now Come With Taglines

Officials from Major League Baseball have agreed to give each player a personal hype-quote — to be chosen by team management, written into the player's contract, and affixed to his name in all broadcasts. The taglines went into effect May 1 for the rest of the season.

Said Major League Baseball spokesman Michael Herson, "TV ratings are down because the fans have lost touch with the players. These taglines are precisely what the public needs to identify with these athletes, to understand the human-interest plot lines that make them worth watching."

Said veteran play-by-play man Jon Miller before the start of Friday night's Mets/Giants game: "Are you kidding? I can't read these things."

But read them he did, by order of the league office.

"And up to the plate steps Carlos Beltran," said Miller in the top of the first inning, before sighing and reluctantly adding: "He's young, he's hip, he's in your face . . . and he might just break your heart!"

In the bottom of the first, Miller, who has been calling Giants games for years on KNBR radio, had to reintroduce the team's biggest star to the Bay Area faithful: "And here comes Barry Bonds . . . the moody thriller everyone is talking about!"

Throughout the Major Leagues, veteran broadcasters struggled to incorporate these mandated marketing campaigns into their broadcasts.

Particularly distracting for announcers is the musi-

> ## "And up to the plate steps Carlos Beltran. He's young, he's hip, he's in your face . . . and he might just break your heart!"

cal soundtrack required for some. As the weepy strings cue, Joe Buck tells a maudlin tale: "He's suffered through divorce, addiction, and the indignity of being traded five times in a seven-year career. His name is Mike Breck, and he takes the mound here in the sixth inning."

Said Tim McCarver, "This is a complete disgrace to our profession. I've never been told what to say, let alone how to say it. And most of these things shamelessly sugarcoat reality. I mean, does anyone still believe that Alex Rodriguez is 'fun for the whole family, good wholesome entertainment—like Magic Johnson, without the tragic twist'?"

Players seem equally dismayed. Said Randy Johnson, "Announcers used to refer to me as a five-time Cy Young Award winner; now it's 'Mount Randy.' Look, just because I'm 6'10" doesn't mean I'm some circus freak. 'You've never seen fastballs hurled at such an altitude'? Give me a break."

Meanwhile, younger players resent that their taglines often compare them to older, more familiar reference points. Says Marlins rookie Josh Davis, "I really don't appreciate being called 'the next Nolan Ryan.' I'm my *own* product." ■

Overtime Game Halted Due To Overtime Pay Dispute

Lakers refuse to finish unless paid time-and-a-half

With the score knotted at 97 at the end of regulation, the January 25 Seattle SuperSonics home game was stopped when the visiting Los Angeles Lakers refused to take the court for the five-minute overtime period.

"I worked Christmas," said Laker guard Devean George en route to the locker room. "I ain't punching in for a bonus shift unless I'm getting an extra vacation day."

In the event of a tie, NBA rules mandate a five-minute overtime period. Should the score remain tied after that, another five-minute period begins, and so on, until one team emerges victorious.

"In theory, this could go on forever," said Kwame Brown. "Imagine finding out that your night's work could continue indefinitely, without even a bathroom break! You think the Teamsters would agree to this?"

Said Chris Mihm: "Tell me—what job in America has absolutely no quittin' time? This is about respect."

A few Lakers singled out National Basketball Players Association representative Billy Hunter for blame, claiming that his poor negotiating skills led to the extra-play-for-no-pay situation.

"Billy, man, he got hoodwinked on this one," said one Laker. "Why would

he agree to a time clock that doesn't punch out?"

With the crowd growing restless, some Lakers offered to continue playing in exchange for nonmonetary remuneration.

Said Lamar Odom, "I'll finish this one, but come the East Coast trip, I'm picking a game and mailing it in, or I'm staying in the hotel."

> ## "Tell me—what job in America has absolutely no quittin' time? This is about respect."

After 45 frantic minutes of negotiation via cell phone, Hunter and Commissioner David Stern agreed to a preliminary overtime pay plan for the NBA. After each Laker and his legal counsel had signed off on the deal, it was agreed that the game would be resumed at a later date, pending a vote by the Players Association.

Leaving the arena, some players still seemed incensed. "I work salary, I don't work overtime," said Kobe Bryant as a valet silently handed him the keys to his Bentley before scurrying off. "Outsource my job to Mexico if you want, because there are some things a working man won't stoop to." ■

Rookie Hits Game-Winner

Few not thanked

> **"Thanks to . . . Skip for putting me in the lineup. Also, my main man Jesus Christ, because he's the only manager I really play for . . . and to my agent, Gilbert Lewis, and my lawyer, Lewis Gilbert."**

Padres rookie Jeff Matthews led off the bottom of the 12th inning with a home run, giving San Diego an 8–7 victory over Pittsburgh on April 28 at Qualcomm Stadium.

"This is just such a thrill for me," said Matthews, 29. "I'm so glad I could help the team. I want to thank my mom and dad, my little sister Becky, and our Irish setters Patrick and Kelly. And my high school coach—this one's for you, Coach Spokes! And all the fans here tonight, they were awesome. And the plate umpire—he could have punched me out on that one-and-two curveball. That was huge.

"Thanks to the Padres' front office for giving me a chance with the big club. And Skip for putting me in the lineup. Also, my main man Jesus Christ, because he's the only manager I really play for. And a special thanks to my agent, Gilbert Lewis, and my lawyer, Lewis Gilbert. And, just, thanks to everyone who's helped me and inspired me along the way. Particularly Reverend Moon. And my bro God. Also Barry Larkin—he was my favorite player growing up, he's the one who made me want to be a ballplayer.

"Oh, and before I forget—I'd like to send a shout-out to the dark knight Lucifer. You the man! And the gals from Destiny's Child, and all our troops in Iraq. But mostly I just want to thank everyone who helped make this night possible. You know who you are! I love you! But we can't forget that there are people all over the world suffering and dying. Let's take a moment of silence to appreciate that," he said, his tone growing somber.

Wiping away a tear, Matthews concluded: "Last but not least, I just want to say, this is for the children! Kids, you can do anything you set your mind to. If you just work hard, and keep walking with Christ, and the Devil, and Dr. Scholl's gel-cushioned insoles—anything can happen." ■

Where we spotlight those who talk about those who do

The following was broadcast on WDAP 1320 AM New York.

Arm Wrestling Goes Professional

Welcome, friends, to the World Professional Arm Wrestling Championships in New York City, the upper-appendage grudge match of the year, the Grapple in the Big Apple—featuring Tricepatops.

[*Cheers*]

Versus the challenger, the Stun Gun from Oregon, Jack the Gripper!

[*Boos*]

Jack is 48 pounds of can-crushing, stress-ball-shredding man-beef. Look at those veins! Get a load of those biceps straining to pop the skin! Are those hands or oven mitts? Look out, folks, we might have a new champ before the day is through. Jack the Gripper is being led in on the shoulder of his owner, Victor Driver, a fireman from Queens. Jack has 22 wins against just one loss.

And now, Ladies and Gentlemen, the moment you've been waiting for, the WPAW champion of the armed world, the Wing of Sting, the Stoic Heroic from the Paleozoic: TRICEPATOPS!

[*Cheers*]

With a 45–2 record and a winning streak approaching 17 matches, Tricepatops is the most feared limb in pro wrestling. He holds two title bracelets. Twice he has ripped arms completely out of their sockets. And he is being led in on the arm of John Henry Thomas, nightclub bouncer from Champaign, Illinois.

[*Cheers*]

Now, as we say before every WPAW match . . . someone's gonna go out on a limb here! ∎

POLL RESULTS

When Did Major League Baseball "Jump the Shark"?

- **Season 38, Episode 1 (1876)**
Chicago Cubs introduced as "pathetic neighbor" character, à la Larry from *Three's Company*. (31%)

- **Season 123, Episode 14 (1961)**
Sandy Koufax brought in as "Jewish superstar" character. (Plot twist proves too far-fetched for viewing public. Koufax written off show after just six seasons.) (14%)

- **Season 143, Episode 3 (1981)**
Lovable minority character "Fernando" introduced to boost low ratings. (37%)

- **Season 157, Episode 1 (1995)**
After '94 strike cancels World Series, producers double number of home runs to win back fans. (Marks end of era, as TV's longest-running dramatic series is retooled into sitcom.) (18%)

Sex Is A Sport If You Do It Rough Enough

First of all I want to thank everyone for all the great feedback on the blog—ever since I got that mention in *Fitness & Wellness* the mail's been pouring in! Extra special thanks to Kate in Roanoke, Va., for the low-fat brownies recipe—you're right, it's hard to believe they're low-fat!

Regarding last week's entry, "Ab-Fab Abs," many of you wrote in with the same question: How in the world does a working person find time for 300 crunches every day? So this week I want to talk about MAKING TIME FOR FITNESS.

Like many young urban professionals, I've got a very busy life: a high-pressure job, lots of great girlfriends, an exciting city to explore . . . With so much going on, finding the time for exercise is almost as much of a challenge as the exercise itself. I get to the gym twice a week, but working in an office 70 long hours like I do, that isn't always enough.

In addition to being a fitness fanatic I also know a thing or two about time management, and I've always looked for creative ways to exercise during everyday life. For example, while carrying my groceries home, I do wrist curls with the bags—fantastic for the triceps. Sometimes, if the bags are heavy enough, I'll even do full bicep curls—when I do, my neighbors here in Chicago look at me like I'm crazy. And believe me, in this town that's saying something!

Fortunately there are all sorts of creative ways for today's working women to burn those calories and shed that flab. Like butt-sex for example. It's even better for your thighs than a super set of squat thrusts. I'm not one to advocate promiscuity or decadent behavior. But in this crazy modern world there's so much to do and so little time—if physical fitness is a concern for you, I'm here to tell you: The rougher the sex, the better.

If you just lie back and take it missionary, you're barely going to get a workout—from a calorie standpoint, you'd be better off playing Ping-Pong!

Look, a lot of my girlfriends absolutely refuse to give head—they think it's disgusting. Well to be honest I do agree with them, it's pretty gross, but I'll tell you this: In 20 years their faces will be so saggy that they'll all be getting chin tucks. But not me!

Good luck, have fun, and don't get hurt! Next week I'll be comparing tennis and racquetball in terms of calorie-burning efficiency. ■

Lori McLeod is a paralegal and author of our pick for best recent blog, LorisFitness Blog.com

The following was observed at a recent NBA game.

Mind If I Throw Your Chair At The Ref?

'Scuse me, but I was just looking down at the visitor's bench, trying to spot where my beer landed, when I noticed you're sitting on a folding chair. Perhaps I could throw it? No, no—not at you, at the stupid ref! Yeah. The one who made that horrible traveling call. I tell ya, we pay so much for these damn seats they could at least give us more stuff to throw.

Huh? I'm in someone's seat? Sorry. I'll move over. Let me just pick up my beers. Yeah, I paid for a ticket. Where's *my* chair? Oh, I tossed it at a broadcaster in the second quarter. Yeah, that was me! No, no, not the one biting—that's my buddy Doug. He got carried off. I was the guy with the chair. Yeah, and the kicking. Security never saw, I guess. Look—chair is gone, I'm out of ammo, and the game is getting kinda close. Little help?

You wanna think about it? Okay. Let me know though, we only have six minutes left here.

So uh . . . about that chair. Still no?

Hey! Shaq fouled out! How about that seat? Come on! Wait, what's that you're eating, a hot dog? You're done with that, right? I'll just take it then . . .

He's coming this way! Hand me something to throw! Yo Shaq! Hey Superman! Big Aristotle! Can I have your autograph? You're my favorite!

Cal Ripken Jr. Has Missed 1,645 Consecutive Days Of Work

"Ironman" legend at risk from streak of naps, daytime TV

BY J. B. GALISHAW

When Cal Ripken Jr. punched the clock a record-breaking 2,632 games in a row for the Baltimore Orioles, he heard nothing but praise and tribute across this great nation of ours, and deservedly so. But the way this guy has been living in his retirement years is a *disgrace*. Sure, Ripken devotes four days a week to his charitable causes, his youth baseball clinics, and running his minor league team, the Aberdeen IronBirds. But what about the rest of the time?

My father, God bless him, worked the graveyard shift at a rendering plant until he was 65. Ripken, on

> ## My father, God bless him, worked the graveyard shift at a rendering plant until he was 65.

the other hand, hasn't worked a salaried day since 2001. As I wrote at the time of Ripken's retirement, if you're a 19-time All Star who's worked over 2,600 games in a row, you've earned the right to take some time for yourself.

But not five years.

Five years of an industrious second career hanging drywall, say, or running a machine shop would be commendable, but it seems as if Ripken's post-retirement goal is to mold a six-foot, four-inch depression into his rec room couch.

Once upon a time, Ripken embodied the principles of clean living, studiousness, and respect for the game that had earned him the nickname "Ironman." You still want to call this shlub an Ironman? An Ironman does not, on a Wednesday, play with his kids and monitor his investments online until noon, before heading to the gym for a game of pickup basketball. An Ironman does not leave the office one day at age 41—41!—and check out for good.

When the full story is written about Cal Ripken Jr., it will surely include the fact that he smacked over 3,000 hits and didn't miss a single day of work from May 1982 until September 1998. But, in the interest of fairness, it should also include the fact that he hasn't missed *The Price Is Right* lately either.

I'm afraid that we in the press—and I'm as guilty as anyone—were too quick to judge Cal Ripken Jr. Maybe some athletes are role models. But not this one. ■

J. B. Galishaw is our senior editor and the author of Pansy in Polyester: The Modern Ballplayer.

Tests Reveal Sosa Using Aluminum Bats

Imaging tests conducted on all 76 baseball bats confiscated from Cubs slugger Sammy Sosa have revealed that not one of them is corked, but 63 are made of aluminum.

"I apologize to the fans," explained Sosa, "I was just trying to give them a show."

Apparently, the use of metal bats is common in Major League Baseball.

"Everybody does it," remarked a major leaguer who did not want to be named. "Wood bats are expensive, and we haven't been getting them comped from the batmakers like we used to. I'll bet if you checked every bat in the majors, you'd find 40 percent are aluminum."

Holding one of Sosa's silver bats under a xenon gas lamp, physicist Dr. Arthur Dresden explained, "Aluminum bats can be identified by their metallic sheen and by the loud 'ping' sound made when striking a ball." ■

According to Dr. Dresden's findings, Slammin' Sammy is swingin' steel.

THIS MONTH IN HISTORY

May 29, 1916
Chicago restaurant denies entrance to shoeless, shirtless Joe Jackson.

May 23, 1976
Anti-Defamation League demands Bears shortstop Tanner Boyle apologize to booger-eatin' morons.

VOLUME 100, NO. 7

JUNE

SPORTS MAGAZINE

THE MAGAZINE

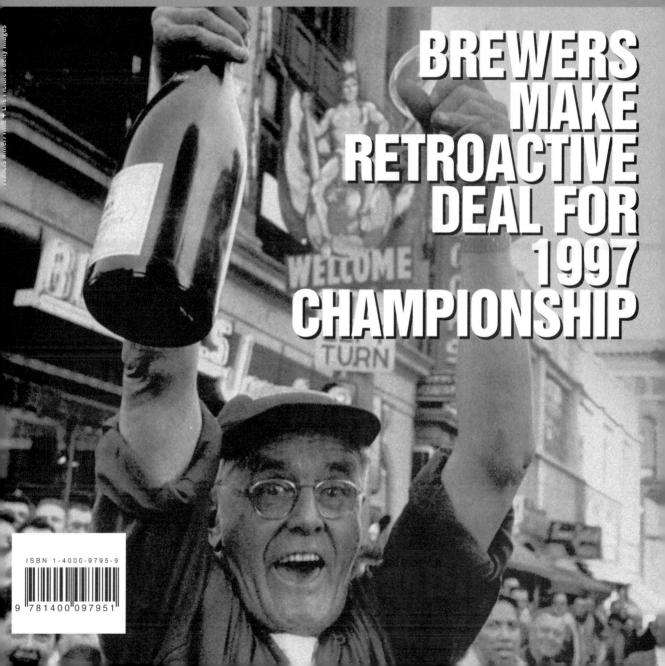

BREWERS MAKE RETROACTIVE DEAL FOR 1997 CHAMPIONSHIP

ISBN 1-4000-9795-9

9 781400 097951

Milwaukee Acquires Past Glory

Florida gets outfielder Brady Clark, 1997 third-place finish, cash

"We're champs?"

asked Madison resident Dana Trumbo upon learning that his favorite team, the Milwaukee Brewers, had just won the 1997 World Series. "Wow! That was such a crappy year too, 1997— like half our team got hurt. This is big news. When's the parade?"

"This is what drives a guy like me to go to work every morning," said Brewers general manager Doug Melvin, beaming and smoking a cigar. "That one deal, that one small edge, which will win a championship. I'm so happy for our fans, for the city. If people don't know about it yet, wait 'til they read the transactions page in tomorrow's sports section."

Terms of the deal are as follows:

"This is a great way for a rust belt city like Milwaukee to win a sports championship— without riots and overturned police cars."

In exchange for the rights to the Marlins' 1997 championship season and all associated pomp, the Brewers surrendered their third-place finish that year, their current starting first baseman, plus an undisclosed amount of cash.

Most Marlins fans did not seem particularly upset by the sudden loss of Florida's first-ever World Series title. Said Shelby Gulla, of Port St. Lucie, "Well, I'll miss reminiscing about Edgar Renteria's clutch hit that won Game 7, of course. That was a wonderful time down here. But third place? For Clark? Not so bad."

Added Gulla's neighbor Tim Tamura, "And anyway, we won another title in '03—for now."

According to financial analyst Marvin Sonneborn, the retroactive exchange is a harbinger of what promises to be a trend: financially strapped sports franchises auctioning past glory for present gain.

"With all the ancillary income a championship provides—highlight videos, T-shirts, memorabilia, even Old Timers' Day—it's a wonder you don't see this more often," said Sonneborn. "I'm not sure you even need to deal a championship. You're telling me the Royals wouldn't sell their strong second-place showing in '89 to bring in a bona fide power hitter right now?"

Brewers owner Mark Attanasio celebrated Milwaukee's first World Series title by spraying champagne all over his office. Said Attanasio, his dark gray suit drenched, "This is a great way for a rust belt city like Milwaukee to win a sports championship—without the riots and overturned police cars, which, as you know, usually result in a higher municipal tax rate. It's a heck of a feeling. I'm going to enjoy this one tonight, because we are finally champs. Tomorrow, it's back to work—this franchise hasn't won anything in over eight years." ■

Baseball Bans Steroids

Stadium vendors to serve only organic hot dogs

In response to mounting pressure from fans and the media, Baseball Commissioner Bud Selig announced what he called a comprehensive plan to remove the taint of anabolic steroids from the Major Leagues.

"The perception persists that our ballparks are filled with artificially inflated products. That's why, starting today, stadium vendors will sell only meats from free-range, completely steroid-free animals.

"Furthermore, as part of our continuing commitment to keep the game pure," continued Selig, "ice cream and shakes available in all 30 Major League

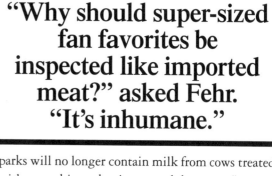

> ## "Why should super-sized fan favorites be inspected like imported meat?" asked Fehr. "It's inhumane."

parks will no longer contain milk from cows treated with recombinant bovine growth hormone."

Reaction by those around the game was largely negative, with Players Association spokesman Donald Fehr vowing that Selig's plan—particularly his intention to perform weekly chemical tests on league hot dogs—would be challenged in court.

"Why should super-sized fan favorites be inspected like imported meat?" asked Fehr. "It's inhumane."

Selig noted that with the game finally free of performance-enhancing additives, attendance might suffer at first.

"Our numbers might drop a bit, as people get used to the idea of a day at the ballpark with no progestin or melengesterol acetate. It might seem like a throwback to the days of boiled peanuts and runs scratched out by sacrifice bunts. But in the end I'm confident the fans will return. Where else can you sit back with a yogurt sundae and a veggie burger and watch dangerously overgrown behemoths swat home runs until their hair falls out?" ■

Big Event Was Probably Lacrosse

In what seems to have been some sort of championship event, or part of a championship series, the Virginia Cavaliers apparently defeated the Johns Hopkins Blue Jays last week in Baltimore, by scoring more points or goals or some such.

Anyhoo, a guy named John Christmas, playing a position where he carried a short metal pole, got a late score by flinging the ball (puck?) into the net, just beyond the reach of a Blue Jay player who may or may not have been a goaltender (guy's pole had a huge webbed area, looked like a pool skimmer).

On that play, Christmas ran right by another opponent who wielded a pole only slightly shorter than a javelin. The guy with the pool skimmer for the Cavaliers, Johnson (Jackson?), seemed to play well, but he stayed within a small circle near the Virginia net, so he might have been serving a penalty, or perhaps been an equipment manager assigned to retrieve the ball.

Insiders say Virginia won 9–7. The Cavaliers certainly jumped around and yelled a lot, so at the very least they're ahead in a best-of-something series. This was most likely the championship round, but it may have been the semifinals. ∎

Ralph Westergard, NBA Scout— Personal Diary

Jan. 3, 2004

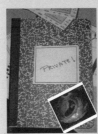

10:30 A.M.: Jefferson High School. Here to see sophomore hoops sensation Jonathan Joseph. JJ is 20 minutes late for workout-- DRUGS? Waiting around, talking with cute volleyball coach, turns out we're from same town. Still no sign of JJ, check messages. JJ finally shows up, works out for 20 minutes, signs autographs for 15. Good jump shot, handwriting needs work.

Pro: Still young. Con: Possibly past his prime.

12:30 P.M.: Lafayette Elementary School, again. One of only four scouts at recess, all here to witness 5'9" center Barney "Rubble" Hathaway, highly regarded third grader.

Pro: Multisport athlete (also plays hopscotch). Con: Already signed with Grizzlies.

2:00 P.M.: O'Flanagan's. Frustrated by usual assortment of grade school pros and high school has-beens. Read newspaper on barstool. Scan birth announcements for exceptionally large babies. Call information for volleyball coach's phone number. Play darts.

5:15 P.M.: Municipal Downs. Word of promising 2-year-old speedster Jack B. Nimble. Reports are accurate: has excellent speed.

Pro: Quick enough to play point guard. Con: Not human.

9:15 P.M.: Bridgeport Hospital. Long night ahead. Viewing several promising sonograms.

Athlete Promoted Solely For Media Skills

Blue Jays catcher long on camera-friendly anecdotes, short on tangibles

Judson Foote, newly promoted catcher for the Toronto Blue Jays, has one thing you can't coach: a complete lack of athletic talent. He hardly ever puts a ball in play, and as a backstop he functions more like a backslow, balls ricocheting off his chest protector more often than lodging in his glove. Yet Foote is in the majors thanks to his prodigious media skills.

"Look—we're struggling at the gate, we're struggling in the field," says Blue Jays GM J. P. Ricciardi. "I'm not going to lie to you. Foote is a good-looking kid, and he knows how to work a room."

Blond, toothy, and handsome, Foote is a natural raconteur who has charmed even the beat reporters with his low-key approach to his .074 bat-

ting average. Foote has recently been named one of the 20 most eligible bachelors in Toronto by *Toronto Magazine.*

Says Blue Jays roving media instructor Peter Schwabacher, "Baseball is in third place in Toronto, after hockey and curling. Having an affable, chatty guy like Foote on the team—even though he might not hit the ball or throw out runners—helps us win promotional tie-ins with local businesses and ups attendance. His numbers on the field may be low, but his Q rating is off the charts." ∎

> # Blond, toothy, and handsome, Foote is a natural raconteur who has charmed even the beat reporters with his low-key approach to his .074 batting average.

Our correspondents keep their ears open and their recording devices on

The following was observed in a Major League locker room last month.

Matt Miller, Pitcher: "Yes Comment"

Q Matt, it seemed like your breaking stuff wasn't really working for you today, so you relied heavily on your fastball—especially in the later innings. Do you think that's what enabled the Rangers to come back from four runs down to tie the game in the eighth?

A Whoa there, Fred, I don't really appreciate your line of questioning. I mean, we're just getting started here, right, people? Let's ease up. No need to go negative.

Q Well, which pitch would you say was working best for you tonight?

A I think my slider, for most of the game. But again, is that really what people want to hear about? I've been trying for weeks to talk about my sexual transgressions, but all you guys ever want to ask me about is fastball, slider, curve. It's enough already.

Q Matt, this was a big win for the ball club—you guys have won five of your last six games, and you're playing as well as you have all season long. Is the feeling around the clubhouse that you can make a run for the playoffs, at least as the wild card?

A Isn't that a bit personal? Let's keep this clean, okay? I mean, how come nobody ever brings up the handgun that was found in my car five years ago? Or my recurring tax fraud problems? It's all "What have you done between the lines?" It's shameful.

Q Matt, why all the secrecy surrounding the identity of the accuser in your sexual assault trial in January?

A I'm glad you asked, Roger. It's an interesting story. See, there was some confusion regarding the age of consent laws in South Carolina, where the trial occurred: Minors' names can't be released, and although she was 18 at the time of the trial, she wasn't at the time of the incident in question.

Q Matt, right before tonight's game you had a chance to meet one of your heroes, pitching legend Nolan Ryan. Can you describe what that was like?

A What is this, a witch hunt? Look, people, I'm not here to talk about today's game, I'm here to talk about my personal problems.

Our correspondents are always on the lookout for noteworthy sports artifacts

The following e-mail was intercepted by our operatives last month.

Subject: Guerrilla Campaign To Promote America's Team

From: Adam Amoroso
To: Jerry Jones

Jerry—

Howdy, cowboy, don't delete! Believe me, I know what ails you: Merchandise sales are down, season tickets for the new stadium aren't moving as fast as hoped, and that upstart football squad down in Houston has loosened your grip on fans in the great state of Texas. Taken together, the 'Boys don't have the buzz they used to. If I could paint your predicament on a lunchboard, it'd say Fans Wanted. Am I right?

To reach today's jaded, increasingly media-savvy consumers, you need to cut through the clutter. Roger Staubach on a billboard in Ft. Worth? Been there. Cheerleaders-at-the-hospital feature on the local newscast? Yawn. The tried is not the true. To return the Cowboys to their rightful glory, you need an under-the-radar, cutting-edge, guerrilla marketing program. Allow me to explain.

It works like this. Say you and I go out for a beer. Maybe we go to a hotspot downtown. See that blonde hottie in the tight dress? She's what we call an alpha, a trendsetter—the popular kid in high school, the person who everyone wants to be. She's also on our payroll. And who's she covertly talking up, to her friends and to all those guys buying her drinks? You got it: the Dallas Cowboys.

Leaders create followers, it's as simple as that. It's subtle, it's smart, most of all—it works. Pretty soon, people are talking, "Hey, what time's the Cowboys game this Sunday?" And buzz begats more buzz. Our approach has worked wonders for clients such as Jones Soda Co. and Orbitz.com.

Quite simply, if you want to build fans for life (with all the merchandise purchases that a devotion to silver and blue entails: team jerseys, Visa cards, star logo baby bibs, etc.), you gotta build a life for fans. Guys see a chubby loser in the back of the bar wearing Zubaz and an Aikman jersey—they look elsewhere for their football team. Maybe they start following the Titans.

That's why the Cowboys have to be positioned as an "aspirational" team. Something we can all hope to be a part of. But this has to be done quietly, so that only those in the know, know about how many yards Julius Jones gained last week against the Saints. You laugh, but it worked for Half.com and Pabst.

One thing is for sure: Fans don't follow certain teams because of their performance on the field. If that were the case, Wrigley Field would be a dustbowl. Fans follow certain teams because it's cool. My older brother was a New York Giants fan, so I became one too. Had I known back in '86 that he was getting paid to talk up Phil Simms at the dinner table—it wouldn't have bothered me one bit.

Look, Jerry, defense may win championships, but buzz wins fans. Hire us, and we'll see to it that all of the nation's water-cooler talk centers around DeMarcus Ware.

Think about it. Your business needs growth. How else you gonna reach new fans? Spam? The Raiders tried it, got them nothing but lawsuits.

Drop me a line.
Yours,
Adam Amoroso
Propeller Marketing
America's #1 Viral Promotions Firm

NEWS

FAKE·A·WISH Foundation Helps Marginal Players Feel Good

Feigned devotion by terminally ill brings star treatment to also-rans

"I want to meet [Mariners reserve outfielder] Eric Simmons!" chirps 12-year-old multiple sclerosis sufferer Rickey Alvarez, reading from a typed script into the telephone.

On the other end of the line Simmons, a career minor leaguer with only 13 games of Major League service, is smiling.

"Hey, kid! You've been watching the M's? You've seen me there on the bench? That's great!"

The truth is no—Alvarez had never heard of Simmons until today. But after some amiable chatting—for which Alvarez has been paid $250—an agreement is reached to have Simmons visit Alvarez in the hospital the next time the Mariners come to Kansas City, should Simmons still be with the team. It's all part of the two-year-old Fake-a-Wish Foundation's plan to improve Simmons's confidence without Simmons's knowledge. The program is quietly being paid for by Mariners management.

"We've tried everything with Simmons—winter ball, personal hitting coaches, you name it—but he still struggles against Major League pitching," said one team official. "Deep down, he doesn't feel like he belongs in the bigs. But granting a wish for some random kid with a life-threatening medical condition and who, with his one last request, 'just wants to meet the great Eric Simmons'—that can really help a guy's swing."

"We make dreams come true," says Fake-a-Wish founder and CEO Barry Shubitz. "Big league dreams."

According to Shubitz, his thriving enterprise has enhanced the on-field performance of dozens of professional athletes.

"We're in the self-esteem business," he says. "We work with ten-dayers, waiver-wire weevils, practice-squad meat puppets, and other fringe players forever on the bubble. Most of these guys, they don't have the groupies, the bestselling jerseys, and the boxes and boxes of fan mail. You see it in their play: no mojo. We give 'em the star treatment, for a fee." ∎

Game Recap: Padres 3, Originality 0

BY MAX MAYOU

Tonight's game between Milwaukee and San Diego was all right if you like that kind of thing.

It wasn't bad per se; it was just way too much of a Stereolab rip-off for my tastes.

I mean, maybe high school kids were impressed, but for those of us who have been listening to indie rock since the '80s, it wasn't much of a ballgame.

The first four innings lumbered along at an almost unbearable pace. Stare, pitch, spit . . . Stare, pitch, spit . . . I'm all for building tension with subtle, monotonous riffs, but Sonic Youth—to name just one obvious example—was doing that kind of thing back in '88.

Things picked up a bit in the fifth inning, when Ryan Klesko and Brian Giles hit back-to-back homers to put the Padres ahead, 2–0. But that abrupt outburst felt glaringly inconsistent with the first half of the game—pointless eclecticism. It's the sign of an insecure outfit that they can't stick to one sound over the course of a nine-inning game. Sudden shifts

> ## . . . for those of us who have been listening to indie rock since the '80s, it wasn't much of a ballgame.

in tempo and volume may have worked for the Pixies, but not everybody has the panache to pull it off.

As the inning resumed and the game returned to its earlier minimalism, the home-run bacchanal felt even more cheap and indulgent.

In the top of the seventh, with the Padres clinging to a 2–0 lead, Giles made a sensational, acrobatic grab of a potential home run off the bat of Geoff Jenkins. The crowd went wild, giving Giles a standing ovation—but I just sat there with my arms folded. Sorry if I can't feign enthusiasm for something like that, but to me the whole display just smacked of effort. You're trying way too hard, man.

But the late innings are where this game really went awry. The seemingly constant stream of relief pitchers felt like a bad gimmick. I mean, what's the point? You might as well stick a blaring saxophone solo into the final moments of an acoustic Nick Drake ballad.

Look, the Padres are a good team, I'm not denying that. They'll finish over .500, and if they add another quality pitcher they could even contend for the division. I just like their older stuff better.

Final score: San Diego 3, Milwaukee 0. Padres pitcher Woody Williams threw a no-hitter. ∎

Max Mayou, of Brooklyn, N.Y., is a freelance music critic and the author of our pick for best recent sports blog, BornOnTheMayou.com

HEY SPORTS FANS!

Are you COMPLETELY OBSESSED with sports? Need to see EVERY INNING your team plays, plus CONSTANT STREAMING FOOTAGE of all the games around the majors? Do you crave UP-TO-THE-MINUTE off-season NFL injury reports? Want to be able to watch EVERY PTA, WTA, PGA, and LPGA EVENT throughout the year, LIVE?!

Do you find yourself CONSTANTLY SWITCHING CHANNELS between two simultaneous games, all the while listening to a third on satellite radio? And then checking online fantasy stats during commercial breaks?

Are you frustrated that the cable sports networks don't offer COMPLETE, COMPREHENSIVE COVERAGE of such CRUCIAL EVENTS as the Winter X Games and National Spelling Bee?

Would you like LIVE UPDATES from the WORLD SERIES OF POKER sent AUTOMATICALLY to your BLACKBERRY or other WIRELESS DEVICE anytime your favorite player RAISES?

How about OVER 200 CHANNELS of sports programming, including TALK-RADIO SHOWS from ALL 50 STATES? Does that sound like a DREAM COME TRUE?

Then GET A FUCKING LIFE.

This message brought to you by the National Literacy Council.

I Greatly Enjoy ESPN's Irreverent, In-Your-Face Style

BY ROBERT GRAEF

As I settle into my golden years, I find I can tolerate precious little in today's popular culture. To this graying observer, nearly all of it is tasteless, vulgar, and narcissistic, from rap "music" to the clothing that teenagers wear.

One glaring exception is ESPN, and in particular its *SportsCenter* program.

I rarely engage the idiot box, but I make a point of watching *SportsCenter* whenever it is on (11 times a day). These anchors astound me with their rapid-fire wit, their comprehensive coverage of a sprawling sports world I stopped following decades ago, and their countless references to the pop culture I so abhor.

Back in my day, sportscasters wouldn't ham it up for the cameras or crack wise; they'd just do their job and tell it like it was. Those guys were more boring than church.

But these anchor-gentlemen of the Entertainment and Sports Programming Network, they split my sides with their unconventional manner of description. The other day a player hit a home run, and the anchorman, a Mr. Wingo, described it thusly: SO-AND-SO HAS LEFT THE BUILDING!

I haven't laughed so vigorously since watching the Ernie Kovacs program!

Perhaps my favorite aspect of their programming is the way they relentlessly inundate the viewer with information. Back when Murrow was my newsman, if you

wanted an out-of-town score, you'd have to wait for the next day's newspaper. But today, thanks to ESPN's amazing "bottom line" feature, you get constant updates of scores, trade rumors, and criminal proceedings scrolling across the game you're trying to watch.

What brilliant visionary thought of this feature, which prevents us from ever settling into the here-and-now?

In a word? Marvelous! ■

> ## Back in my day, sportscasters would just do their job and tell it like it was. Those guys were more boring than church.

Robert Graef, 66, is a retired actuary in Scottsdale, Ariz.

Yo, ESPN Is Wack, Yo

BY CHARLES WING

SportsCenter? That shit is weak, son. Mad weak! Can I get some love for the announcers who kicked it out 30 years ago? I'm talkin' 'bout cats like Heywood Broun, Vin Scully, Jim McKay. Can I get a WHAT-WHAT for Red Barber? Man, I miss the old school, which I've seen on ESPN Classic.

Way backbackback then it was all about the subtle, no rebuttal. You feel me? When Billie Jean was King, so was understatement.

These dudes on *SportsCenter* are stone-cold HATIN' on the purity of the games. Holla at me if you got the love for journalistic integrity!

And yo, what's the dizz-eal with these lickety-quick highlights and jump cuts? What, do we all got A.D.D.? You trippin', cousin.

And WAZZAP with these lingo-slingin' anchors? With the ill skillz today's ballers got, there ain't no need to get cute with the description. I asked for highlights and the final score, not a *South*

> **Way backback-back then it was all about the subtle, no rebuttal. When Billie Jean was King, so was understatement.**

Park reference and a P-Funk lyric. Dawg, you tryin' way too hard.

In a word? Wack. ■

Charles Wang, 17, is a student in Hyattsville, Md.

Charles Wang, 17, is a student in Hyattsville, Md.

NEW MAJOR LEAGUE BASEBALL PROMOTIONAL EVENTS

• **Bat Day:** All fans 12 and under will receive a live Central American spear-nosed bat, suitable for cultivating guano.

• **Kids Night:** Nine innings of roving promotional T-shirt cannon, with a brief break in the fifth for baseball.

• **Turn Back The Clock Night:** Thrill to baseball in the 1920s. Players will wear woolen uniforms, hot dogs will reflect pre-FDA ingredients, and concession stands will revisit 1925 prices. Bleacher seats reserved for Negro and Irish patrons.

• **Fan Appreciation Day:** All fans will be strongly encouraged to appreciate today's game.

Baseball Is A Game Of Failure

Especially when you suck

BY EVAN ARKO

It's been said that part of baseball's appeal lies in the fundamental failure at the heart of the game. Consider: As a batter, succeeding a quarter of the time is respectable, and succeeding a third of the time is something only the best hitters achieve. Now consider this: What if you succeeded an eighth of the time?

Now imagine, just for a moment, that a player who succeeds one-eighth of the time is doing it at the lowest rung of professional baseball. And imagine, if you will, that at one point, barely two years ago, he had reached a much higher rung—the rung right below the Major Leagues, in fact—and at that rung he was doing great: succeeding well over a quarter of the time but not quite a third of the time. 29.2 percent of the time to be exact. With 14 homers and 23 stolen bases.

"The numbers don't lie: Baseball is a very hard game."

Now imagine that this promising young player—who was an excellent defensive outfielder too, by the way—was snowboarding in the off-season. And that he tried to impress this cute girl who went to UC-Santa Cruz with a sick aerial move, and he dislocated his hip. And he never fully recovered, and his skills diminished, and he was demoted to the lowest rung, and even at that rung he managed to succeed only an eighth of the time. Or after last night's game, more like a ninth of the time.

The numbers don't lie: Baseball is a very hard game.

Or look at strikeouts. Watch a Major League game, and you'll routinely see All Star–caliber players flailing at pitches in the dirt. In fact, the average major leaguer strikes out about once every other game, and many free-swinging sluggers strike out once a game or more. With those odds, can I be blamed for striking out three times last night, twice with the bases loaded? And making two errors?

It's no wonder Ted Williams said that hitting a baseball is the single hardest thing to do in all of sports. It's just a wonder he said it with a lifetime batting average of .344. ■

Evan Arko is a reserve outfielder for the Cedar Rapids (A) Kernels.

Mineshaft: Sorenstam Doesn't Belong At Suffolk Downs

In a press conference last month, Mineshaft told reporters that Annika Sorenstam, the world's no. 1 female golfer, has "no business" competing in the upcoming James B. Moseley Breeders' Cup Handicap, held at Suffolk Downs.

"I don't know what she's trying to prove, but she just doesn't belong here. Women have their own events. For that matter, so do men."

Mineshaft also said he hoped that Sorenstam would "break a leg and then get shot," but he later apologized and said the statement had been taken out of context.

All eyes have been on Sorenstam recently, as she prepares to be the first female golfer in over 50 years to compete in an NTRA event.

Sorenstam, of Stockholm, Sweden, said that despite all the media attention, she has encountered mostly respect and civility from her newest competitors. "I'll get a stern glance here and there, an occasional snort, but nobody says much." ∎

THIS MONTH IN HISTORY

June 17, 1527
Charles V credited with half-sack of Rome.

June 5, 1960
Ted Williams announces he will retire to "spend more time with The Kid."

VOLUME 100, NO. 8

JULY

SPORTS MAGAZINE

THE MAGAZINE

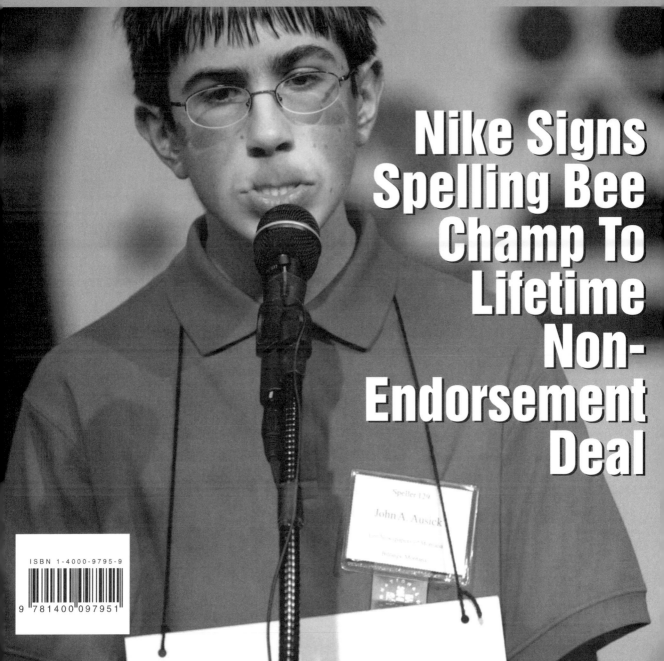

Nike Signs Spelling Bee Champ To Lifetime Non-Endorsement Deal

ISBN 1-4000-9795-9

9 781400 097951

$4.3 Million Agreement Ensures Gawky 8th Grader Will Never Wear Company Apparel

Outbidding rivals Reebok and Fila, Nike has signed 13-year-old Melvin Peh to a multiyear non-endorsement contract, ensuring the gangly teen will never be seen wearing the company's clothing.

Peh was approached by Nike officials last week, after outlasting 251 competitors to win the annual Scripps National Spelling Bee. The Minneapolis native won the $12,000 grand prize, along with an encyclopedia and a trophy, by correctly spelling the word *mangonel*.

"I was watching on cable, half paying attention," explained Nike founder and CEO Phil Knight, "when I saw this Spock-eared nerdlinger asking about Latin or Greek origins. The camera zoomed in, and that's when I saw the swoosh on his T-shirt. I about had a heart attack."

The agreement ensures Peh will wear only non-Nike apparel for life, or until the company no longer makes products targeted at his age group.

"This is a great opportunity," said Nike spokesperson Pamela Benanav. "Melvin's one of the most talented spellers in years, and an avid violinist. Tests place him in the top half of one percent of all eighth graders in math. Just the sight of this spelling prodigy bounding to chess club practice in a pair of tightly cinched, double-knotted Air Zoom Ultraflights could undo a dozen marketing campaigns."

Nike's betting millions that Peh will remain tremendously unpopular as he matures.

"He's only 13, so there's so much potential. And with puberty just around the corner, we think the worst is yet to come. We're not always right on who we don't endorse, but we like our chances without Melvin." ∎

LOST & FOUND

Our correspondents are always on the lookout for noteworthy sports artifacts

The following was found at a recent autograph-signing event at the Mall of America in Bloomington, Minn.

Autograph Signing Term Sheet--Jesus Of Nazareth

I. The Almighty will sign for exactly two hours, no exceptions.

II. Promoter/venue must provide signing table, five (5) pens (felt-tip only, no ball point), and one (1) padded and height-adjustable office chair, of Herman Miller Aero or similar design.

III. Promoter/venue must provide bottled water (un-holy okay) for Jesus and support staff.

IV. At least one week before the event, promoter/venue will post the following instructions in a highly visible location:

Greetings, Christ fans! Jesus loves that you came here today. Please be aware of the following rules:

All items intended for signature will be subject to the following:

    Flat Items: $75
    Other Items: $100
    8" X 10" Last Supper Print, Includes
    Autograph: $225

While the Son of God is signing your item, brief, encouraging words are acceptable. However, please be respectful of those behind you in line; do not attempt to engage Christ in conversation.

Please do not approach Christ with items including bobbleheads, Notre Dame jerseys or the like, or anything bearing the signature of John The Baptist, or any of the apostles, as Jesus does not sign team balls.

The Almighty will not sign any relics, including shrouds or pieces of the True Cross, nor any relic replicas, or photographs of said relics.

As this has caused problems in the past, please do not ask the Holy Son to draw personal messages or stigmata on your person.

Do not ask Jesus for carpentry or wagering tips.

One signature per patron, please.

Name
Organization
Signature
Date
2/3/66k

Name
Organization
Signature
Date
2-3-6

NEWEST SPORTS CHANNELS

- **T$C**—The Salary Channel

- **NFL Network 2**—Erudite, Dry, Coldly Schtickless Football Analysis

- **ESPNSports**—Showing Actual Sporting Events

- **OOPSNET**—The Apology Network

- **!H!**—Hype TV

All-Star Game Rendered Even More Important

Winner to earn home-field advantage, appliances, more

Major League Baseball's upcoming All-Star Game will be its most meaningful ever. Spurred by 2003's infamous tie game, the commissioner's office introduced a plan to restore significance to the contest: The league that won the Midsummer Classic was rewarded with home-field advantage in the World Series. Not happy with the level of play this incentive induced, the commissioner has revamped the winner's reward yet again: This year the league that wins the game will get "do-overs" on any two Series plays and an assortment of practical, rust-resistant prizes.

The winner will also have the option to trade one of the Series do-overs for a clubhouse visit from a surprise celebrity guest. Furthermore, the MVP of the All-Star Game and the winner of the Home Run Derby will face off in a biathlon for a reality sports show

premiering on Spike-TV this fall.

Commissioner Bud Selig issued this statement: "It's time to put the fierce competitive edge back in this game. Fans want to see the players fighting for something. And this year they will, whether that something is home-field edge for the two or three players who will make it to the World Series or, for the remainder of the participants, a washer/dryer."

Angels skipper Mike Scioscia, the manager of the American League All-Star team for the tie game and a player when the annual midsummer battle was fought to the death simply for the glory, echoed the accolades for the commissioner heard around the league. "Selig is absolutely right: In recent years, the players have lost their competitive drive, their hunger to excel in the All-Star Game. Like 2003, when they fought tooth and nail for 11 innings before being ordered to stop." ∎

Mom-And-Pop America's Cup Team Facing Doubts, Scurvy

Charlie and Gladys Dolger, skipper and chief tactician of the 33-foot *Shazam!,* have encountered repeated hardship in their quest to return sailing's top trophy to the United States.

"If it's not one thing, it's another," explained Gladys, her gums puffy and bleeding from prolonged lack of vitamin C. "First our sponsor, Al's Tackle Box of Huntington Beach, welches on the 150 bucks and the live bait. Then on Friday [$55 million Swiss entrant] *Alinghi* cuts us off rounding the second mark.

"Today I thought we had a lead on [79-foot super-computer-designed] *Team New Zealand* during the first leg, but then Charlie tripped over a cleat and dropped the winch handle overboard. God, I'm hungry."

Since consuming their last piece of fruit—a lemon peel dropped in a cup of collected rainwater—somewhere in the South Pacific during their 8,500-mile voyage from L.A. to the race site off the coast of Spain, the Dolgers have not come close to supplying their

sun-, salt-, and wind-chapped bodies with a sufficient amount of daily nutrients.

Nonetheless, the pair has not given up hope of winning. Despite being out-manned by 15 crew members and 65 support staff per

boat and the only entrant not funded by an international corporate syndicate, Charlie will not yield any advantage. To prevent competitors and spies from viewing the keel design of his 1982 fiberglass pleasure cruiser, the skipper vowed never to make landfall or take on supplies in the Southern Hemisphere; the Dolgers' last visit ashore was a brief stop at a San Diego marina four months ago.

However, there are indications that team unity may be cracking. Gladys recently charted a course that led directly to a seaside restaurant in Valencia. Charlie did not follow it.

"I tried to show him that my bones are thinning by thumping my hand against the mast and holding up the broken fingers," said Gladys, her stomach distended from malnourishment. "But Charlie just kept gnawing at the last bits of stray leather." ■

Baseball Still America's Favorite Sport . . . For Sex Metaphors

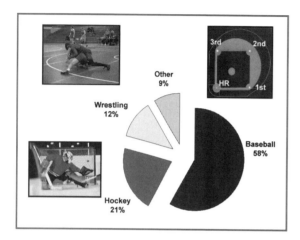

Other
9%

Wrestling
12%

Baseball
58%

Hockey
21%

Despite baseball's decline in popularity over the last 20 years, a new Kinsey Institute study finds that the game is still emphatically Americans' sport of choice when they seek a sly way of referring to sex acts.

"You can say what you want about baseball," said Hofstra sociologist Ben Squire. "You can point out how more people watch football. And basketball, and the X Games, soccer, figure skating, and Texas Hold 'Em. But one thing is certain: 'second base,' 'third base,' and 'going all the way' will never be replaced by confusing expressions like 'hole in one,' 'bank shot,' or 'man in motion.'"

Pro Athlete Goes Back To School

JEFFERSON WILSON, the star NBA forward who left UCLA after his sophomore season for the riches of professional basketball, has decided to return to the classroom.

"It's something I've always had in the back of my mind," said Wilson at a Los Angeles, Calif., press conference. "Something that I always knew I should do. Not just for me, but for my parents and grandparents, who never had the opportunity.

"It's a pride thing, mainly," continued Wilson. "I got unfinished business with the chalkboard. My momma always said, 'I wish you earned a degree.' Well, in eight course hours, Momma, your boy will have his certificate!"

In addition, Wilson will not receive any more points on his driver's license, and he will not be subject to higher car insurance premiums.

Said Wilson's agent, Randy Helstein, "It's wonderful when big-time athletes participate in academia. That's why we are getting the word out here today. I think the message Jefferson and his sponsors, AND1 and Pepsi, are sending to America's children is a vital one: Nobody is too cool for school, no matter if it's high school, vocational school, or the school of hard knocks."

Wilson will be the first in his family to complete traffic school.

The 6'8" Kings standout added that

he intends to enroll in one of the online courses offered by the California Department of Motor Vehicles, thus saving himself from having to attend class.

"My doing 83 in a 55 [mph zone] was wrong. But that's between me and the DMV. Now, if you'll excuse me, I have studying to do."

Chris Berman Honors Negro Leagues

In a ceremony at the Oakdale Cemetery in Franklin, Va., the final resting spot for several Negro League baseball stars, master of ceremonies and ESPN personality Chris Berman addressed the crowd last month.

"Let me begin by saying how honored I am to be here today, and to be a part of such a historic occasion. The great men we celebrate this afternoon represent a sad chapter in American life, that of segregation. But they also represent a virtual treasure trove of untapped nicknames.

"So what are we waiting for? In true 'Shwam' style, we're going to do this as a Top Ten. I am honored to have Negro League legend Buck 'Stops Here' O'Neil by my side.

"Coming in at number ten, we've got former outfield star for the Newark Eagles, Luke Walker. Well, 'Stops Here,' this one was a no-brainer. Clearly this guy should be remembered, forevermore, as 'Sky.' "

Remarked O'Neil, "Luke was called 'Birch Bark'—because they said his skin was tough as birch bark. Had to be, when your whole family had been killed by the Klan like ol' Luke's was."

Berman continued: "I don't know if the guy could jump two inches off the ground, so 'Skywalker' may not be appropriate, but c'mon folks, how could I resist? And everyone loves *Star Wars,* right?"

Walker's widow, Beatrice, 97, had never heard of the film.

"Moving on to number nine . . . number nine . . . number nine . . ." said Berman, "well, this one's too easy: A great second baseman and leadoff hitter for

> **"The great men we celebrate this afternoon . . . represent a virtual treasure trove of untapped nicknames."**

the old St. Louis Stars, it's Bill Summer.

"I could go just about anywhere with this one, right, 'Buck Fifty'? Well, enough suspense. Here we go: It's Bill 'I know what you did last' Summer. I also considered Bill 'Boys of' Summer but that felt too obvious. Gotta give some love to horror flicks."

Reaction to the ceremony was mixed. Said Reginald Hayes, grandson of Indianapolis Clowns pitching ace Spottsford Hayes, "I appreciate ESPN replacing my grandfather's decrepit headstone. But I have to admit, it was a bit strange seeing them drill in the nickname 'Purple.' " ■

Where we spotlight those who talk about those who do

This month we feature color commentator Bill Warren, newest member of the Pennsylvania Sports Broadcasting Hall of Fame.

Pirates v. Nationals

TOM DAYAN: We're back, top of the second inning in Pittsburgh, no score between the Nationals and Pirates. Diller deals, Blaise swings . . . mercy, what a changeup. Blaise was out in front of that one by about a foot and a half. He nearly fell over.

BILL WARREN: Fantastic changeup there—had Blaise completely baffled. You love to see a young pitcher with such command of his offspeed stuff. A lot of young guys have great fastballs but not much else—Diller is showing a maturity far beyond his years. But you know, in order to have a good season, I think the key will be to stay within myself, take things one broadcast at a time, and practice, practice, practice.

TOM: Sure, practice is good. Blaise took a moment to regroup, now he steps back in the box. Diller rears back and fires. Ouch, the heat! Fastball right down Broadway, called strike two.

BILL: Ninety-four on the radar gun.

TOM: Yowza! The kid can fire it.

BILL: Sure can. Reminds me of Mark Prior of the Cubs: big tall stud, smooth mechanics, fluid delivery. The sky's the limit for this kid, and Pirates management is, understandably, very excited about him. I'd like to take this moment to

> ## "In order to have a good season, I think the key will be to stay within myself, take things one broadcast at a time, and practice, practice, practice."

thank the good Lord for giving me the powers of observation and the clear diction necessary to make it in this business. I'm so grateful for the opportunity to be here.

TOM: It's a living. Diller's ahead of Blaise 0-and-2 now, he's got him where he wants him. He sets, he throws. Curveball outside, ball one.

BILL: He's really showing the whole repertoire here. With the dangerous Phil Menton on deck, Diller does not want to let Blaise reach base. The fans here in Pittsburgh have been so great to my family and me. Not only during my trial, but also in that difficult period before the trial had even begun, while the lab was performing the DNA tests on me and the seven other people involved.

TOM: That's nice. The pitch . . . another changeup, and Blaise watches it float by for a called strike three. That excellent changeup again, and there's one out. The vet-

eran Phil Menton steps in—Menton's got a big bat, but a reputation as a volatile personality. There was a clubhouse scuffle with teammate Louis Scott last year, and that well-publicized domestic dispute back when he was playing for Minnesota.

BILL: All true, Tom, all true, but you know, people change. And every time you join a new team it's a new beginning. That's why those remarks I made on WBLN two years ago are something I'd prefer not to talk about. I've made some mistakes in my life—just like everyone—but I've learned from those mistakes and moved on. I've apologized to the fans, and to Boy Scout Troop 113 of Altoona. And to the people of Niger for accidentally mispronouncing their country's name—that was an honest mistake. And I'd been drinking. But if these things keep getting brought up, then I have to keep talking about them. I say let bygones be bygones, and just let a broadcaster do his job. ∎

EX-JOCK
SORT OF COAUTHORS BOOK
ON LEADERSHIP

Former New York/New Jersey Net Mike Jenkins has written a new book on leadership.

IT'S NOT A GAME, IT'S LIFE: HOW TO WIN AT THE GAME OF LIFE
is chock-full of insightful life-lessons from one of the sports world's most independent thinkers and his book-
writing team. Ghostwritten by freelance writer Leonard Ignall, with a foreword by former Knicks 12th man Eddie
Lee Wilkins and an epilogue by Ignall's girlfriend, *It's Not a Game* is a how-to for anyone intent on blazing his or
her own unique trail to the top.

Sprinkled with rich personal anecdotes as told to Ignall by Jenkins's associates, the book mines his 3½ years in the
NBA trenches and subsequent buy-in to a profitable automobile-detailing franchise. In the process, *It's Not a Game*
unearths pearls of wisdom on how to win at everything from basketball to life to personal grooming.

Readers will learn "7 Crucial Steps to Successful Winning," including
• How to Identify and Avoid the 8 Quadrants of Losing
• How to Make the Business of Life Your Business Life
• Why Winning at Pro Basketball and Selling Carpet Cleaner Solvent from a Cubicle Are Exactly the Same
• What Tomorrow's Successful Leaders Are Eating TODAY
• Getting Your Leadership Shit Together

Borrowing liberally from proven leadership texts like Pat Riley's *The Winner Within: A Life Plan for Team Players*
and *Success Is a Choice: 10 Steps to Overachieving in Business and Life* by Rick Pitino, Jenkins's time-tested management
advice is a must for anyone serious about earning a better life-score.

Whether you seek to inspire your company's sales team or simply improve your own life's winning percentage,
It's Not a Game by Jenkins, Ignall, Fulghum, & Chopra is a slam dunk!
Act now—the first 5,000 copies will include Jenkins's autograph hand-stamped on the inside cover.

AVAILABLE WHEREVER BOOKS ARE SOLD.

I'm Looking Forward To Three Years, Fifty Weeks Of Real Wars

BY J. B. GALISHAW

For two weeks every four years, athletes from all over the globe convene for the Olympic Games. Putting aside nationalistic differences, the world does battle with soccer balls, balance beams, and shot puts. Have we lost sight of what really matters?

I mean, if the entire world does one kind of fighting for three years and 50 weeks, then another kind for just two weeks, then back to the first kind for another three years and 50 weeks, and so on . . . well then, doesn't it stand to reason that the first kind of fighting is a LOT more important than the second?

If there were real value to these athletic contests, don't you think we would set aside two weeks every four years to bomb each other into tangy shrapnel, then spend the remaining three years and 50 weeks holding international weightlifting and Ping-Pong competitions?

There's near-constant talk of the significance of these Olympic victories, of "a nation's spirits lifted" by a win in judo or kayaking—but I'm skeptical. I mean, does it go something like this?

"Well, I live in a totalitarian regime, I share a rural shack with eight siblings, the drinking water is almost as clean as industrial nations' urine . . . But on the bright side, someone from the capital city—where I've never been, and never will be—just culminated 10 years of state-funded training by defeating Togo and Luxembourg in archery. Gee, that really lifts

my fucking spirits. Hey, buddy, while you're using that bow and arrow, you think you could catch us something to EAT?"

Which raises a question: Just how many of these events exist only to provide symbolic victories for nations that have no chance at real ones? Are we supposed to weep tears of joy for Brunei because they won one of the eight flat-water canoeing events? Good for Brunei! Maybe next they could gain a military victory. Or a military.

If they add jacks as a medal event in '08, maybe we could have a feel-good moment for the oppressed people of Micronesia. Or perhaps the entire population of Botswana would forget about trifling concerns like famine if they could only earn the bronze in rock-paper-scissors.

While we're at it, why don't we just call the Closing Ceremonies "Everybody's a Winner Day" and give out gold medals for sportsmanship, most improved uniforms, and best national anthem? That'd make these two-bit countries feel all warm and fuzzy as they prepare for 206 weeks of smart bombs and cholera.

All this hoopla over supposed symbolic victories misses the point: If you want a "spiritually uplifting victory" then START A WAR.

J. B. Galishaw is our senior editor and the author of Strawberry Girl: A Coming-of-Age Novel for Young Adults.

Our recurring feature in which we revisit the sports lore of simpler times, via the *SMTM* archives

Pistons' Triumph Has Children Briefly Interested In Teamwork

Fad may last the summer

After the scrappy Detroit Pistons' victory over the star-studded Los Angeles Lakers in the NBA Finals, headlines across the country proclaimed the emphatic message: Team play and hard work can overcome flashy, selfish superstars. Parents, coaches, and NBA officials are optimistic that this concept will resonate with the youth of America for perhaps as long as a month.

NBA commissioner David Stern, attending the NBA's peewee slam dunk competition—in which children aged 6 to 8 perform acrobatic dunks on a 5-foot hoop for a cash prize—remarked:

"Notice how many of these kids are wearing Ben Wallace–style Afros as they hone their predunk victory dances and 360-degree crotch-grabbing slams.

"Clearly, the Pistons' impact is being felt."

Mary Beth Cane of Charlotte, N.C., a mother of three, agreed. "My kids were glued to the screen watching the Pistons pass and pass the ball, and I think they learned something valuable from it. They used to be all 'me me me,' but now they work *together* on their trash-talking."

Said Rockford, Ill., church league basketball coach Brian Millman, "My kids were wearing Pistons jerseys almost as long as they were quoting their favorite lines from the *Garfield* movie."

Ian Weiser of the Center for the Study of Sport in Society noted that this story rang familiar: "This year was eerily reminiscent of the late '80s, when

> "They used to be all 'me me me,' but now they work *together* on their trash-talking."

the same teams squared off, and the 'Bad Boys' Pistons took down the 'Showtime' Lakers. In '89, as in '04, that triumph of blue-collar over glitz, teamwork over star power, resonated profoundly. Until nightfall."

Veteran sportscaster Bob Costas believes that the '04 Pistons have left an indelible mark on sports culture. "We watch our favorite skateboarders shred the half-pipe at the X Games for personal glory. We obsessively track home-run leaders for our fantasy leagues, but we have no idea which real teams are in first place. The Pistons showed America the value of selfless, team-oriented play. We can all learn from this lesson, which has already been forgotten." ■

THIS MONTH IN HISTORY

July 29, 1985
Coach to John Fogerty: "No."

July 22, 2001
Bored Lance Armstrong pops 23-mile wheelie through Pyrenees.

VOLUME 100, NO. 9

AUGUST

SPORTS MAGAZINE

THE MAGAZINE

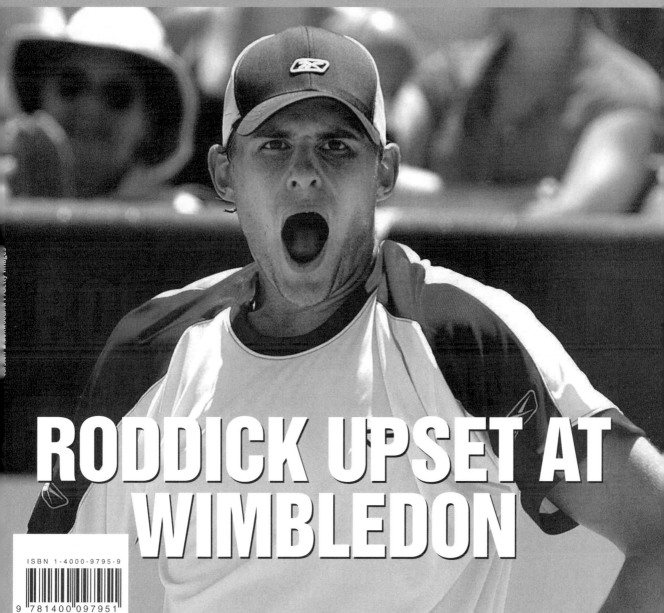

RODDICK UPSET AT WIMBLEDON

ISBN 1-4000-9795-9

9 781400 097951

No. 3 Seed Very, Very Upset

In one of the biggest stories to emerge from Wimbledon so far, American star Andy Roddick was upset in the first round.

Roddick told reporters, "Well for starters, the breakfast at the hotel was brutal. When people think of Wimbledon, they think of strawberries and cream—but the food here is just terrible. I know scones are supposed to be dry . . . but not *that* dry."

Asked to cite factors other than breakfast, the third-ranked Roddick mentioned having to drive on the left side of the road, "girlfriend problems," and also certain aspects of his tennis match against unseeded Stefan Koubek of Austria. "The line judges really got to me. To lose a break point on such a questionable call in the seventh game of the third set—that upset me deeply."

Although this is arguably the biggest setback that Roddick has endured in his career, he feels confident that he can "learn from this" and "move on."

Roddick won the match, 6–2, 6–3, 6–3, and will face Jarkko Nieminen of Finland in the second round. ■

Health Experts Denouncing Cell Phone Games

Advocate return to console systems

The new advent of cell phone video games is causing great concern among today's fitness experts, parents, and educators, who overwhelmingly agree that these games do not provide the benefits of traditional, health-minded activities like arcade games and console systems.

"I may be from the old school," said George Hafner, 41, a father of two, "but back in my day, if we wanted exercise we'd get up and go outside. To the arcade. It was five whole blocks away. And pretty much all the games required standing up, except for that tabletop Ms. Pac Man. I had the high score on that thing for like a year."

Experts agree. "Our research has revealed a very disturbing trend," said Steven Jacobs, president of the National Fitness Insti-

tute, "toward activities that exercise less and less of the participant's body. Console systems like Nintendo and PlayStation raised a whole generation that used nothing but their hands. Now, mobile games are reducing it even further, to just fingertips. What's next, breathing into a tube? I simply cannot overstate the value of activities that exercise the whole body, like tennis or swimming, or one of those auto racing games where you work the gas and brakes with your feet. Like Pole Position. Is that still around?"

But members of the burgeoning mobile gaming industry are quick to defend their product. Said Janel Beaton, 26, a sales representative for Slam-Jam Mobile Games, "Critics warn that these games are far less engaging and stimulating than the classic youth activities of last century, like bas-

ketball and Super Mario Brothers. But times have changed. These days we've all got such busy lives. We need a game you can play with one finger while placing a phone call with the rest of that hand."

Parents are realizing that if they want to steer their children toward activities they consider more beneficial and healthy, they must take an active role.

"It's always a struggle for parents to teach their children values that now seem archaic," said Carol Ruder, 44. "But Tom and I believe in it passionately. For example, we hand-pick quality educational programs for our kids to watch."

She motioned toward the family room, where Phoebe, 15, and Colin, 12, sat slumped on the couch, pretending to watch *Behind the Music: The Go-Go's* while discreetly playing Jewel Quest on their Nokias. ∎

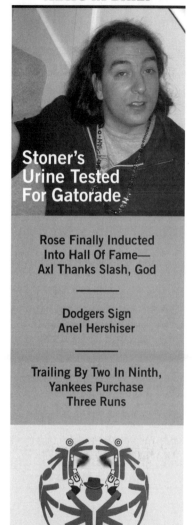

Arthur Ashe, Chris Evert Honored For Lack Of Fashion Sense

The leading stars and scribes of tennis gathered at the International Tennis Hall of Fame in Newport, R.I., last month for a banquet hailing two of America's greatest players. Speakers shared the podium, reflecting on the careers of Chris Evert and the late Arthur Ashe. Some of their remarks:

BUD COLLINS: What can we say about Arthur Ashe? Ambassador of the game. Promoter of social justice. Stoic AIDS sufferer. Frumpy champion.

While many remember Ashe the gentleman, the scholar with the ferocious serve, some of us wonder: Just how successful could he have been with a more fashion-forward approach? Intellectuals admired him, but he might have found a broader fan base had he embraced a bold wardrobe.

VIC BRADEN: Ah, Chrissie Evert.

Ashe: AFP/Getty Images; Evert: Tim Chapman/Getty Images Sport/Getty Images

"Fifty-five consecutive match wins in 1974 and not one memorable catsuit or pair of knee-high boots? Chris Evert, you had one weakness."

The beloved "girl next door" who became champion, winner of 18 Grand Slam singles titles. Blessed with fierce ground strokes and a lethal drop shot, Evert's style, such as it was, never strayed from unimaginative: white skirt, white top, white sneakers. She could just as easily have been a nurse.

JAMES BLAKE: Ashe was the first black man to win the U.S. Open, and he did it without unveiling a single new look for the entire two-week tournament. That says something. It says he didn't know much about promoting the game.

SERENA WILLIAMS: Chrissie's aggressive game inspired me to reach new heights. She won nearly $9 million during her 19-year career—looking back, perhaps some of that money should have gone toward a personal shopper.

MARY CARILLO: Fifty-five consecutive match wins in 1974 and not one memorable catsuit or pair of knee-high boots? Chris Evert, you had one weakness.

DICK ENBERG: The thing I remember most about Arthur Ashe's surprising Wimbledon title in '75 was his stodgy, steel-rimmed eyeglasses. I mean, they had contact lenses back then, you know? Get a clue.

In his stirring autobiography Ashe wrote, "The purest joy in life comes with trying to help others." He could have helped us all by pulling down those white socks.

PAM SHRIVER: Sadly, despite all of the press coverage—heightened by romances with Jimmy Connors and Burt Reynolds—the only trend Evert pioneered was the two-handed backhand.

ANDRE AGASSI: Even after his illustrious tennis career, Ashe never changed. When I saw him on TV protesting U.S. treatment of Haitian refugees just months before his death, I was like, Are you kidding me? Khakis and a panama hat?

Jeanne Moutoussamy-Ashe accepted the accolades on behalf of her late husband. She was clad in a crisp beige Tahari pantsuit.

END ZONE CELEBRATIONS BANNED FOR UPCOMING NFL SEASON

- Spiking the ref

- Leaping into crowd to grab laptop computer, giving PowerPoint presentation on own greatness

- Urinating on cameraman

- Impaling unconscious defender with unlicensed merchandise

- Eating the ball

- Removing contract from sock, waving at owner's suite, demanding on-the-spot renegotiation

- Kneeling, crossing self, giving God the finger

New Coach Pledges Passivity

Conservative offense will play not to lose; defense will read, react, discuss

Brought in to revive a moribund program, new Boise State head football coach Rusty Gucker is looking forward to running things by the book.

"There hasn't been a lot of excitement around here the past few years," explained Gucker, "and I think that's good. When players get excited, they forget their blocking schemes."

Speaking at his first press conference, Gucker described his coaching style.

"On offense, we're not gonna take a lot of chances. Mostly we'll select plays by considering the down and distance, looking up what we usually do in such a situation, and doing it again.

"I don't want to have some wide-open scoring machine that can strike at any moment. I want to win football games. We're gonna run on first down, pass on third, see how it goes.

"On D, we're not gonna get after the quarterback that much. I don't want to get into trouble with offside penalties and such. And I don't want defenders flying around wreaking havoc. Let the opponent take what's theirs. Above all: no mistakes. If you think the play unfolding before you is a run, not a pass, double-check it with a teammate before doing anything brash."

Asked the temperament he was seeking in recruits, Coach Gucker said he was looking for play-ers who are committed to knowing their limits.

"I'm very excited. I can't wait to start scheming new draw plays and working on our fair catches. This team went two-and-nine last year. I don't see why, if everyone plays within themselves, we can't improve on that just a little bit.

> "There hasn't been a lot of excitement around here the past few years," explained Gucker, "and I think that's good. When players get excited, they forget their blocking schemes."

"A lot of new hires start talking about how they're gonna play an aggressive style of D, blitz the heck out of the opposing QB, and throw the ball down the field. That's not my style. I'm more methodical. If we're chasing two scores late, we'll pack it in, save our strength, learn to fight another day, or year." ∎

Athlete Gives Back To Community

Rulon Samuels, star forward for the Golden State Warriors, returned to his blighted hometown of East St. Louis, Ill., last month after a six-year absence. With Ludacris blaring out of his custom stretch Hummer limousine, Samuels rolled into the Emerson Park section of town he once called home and unloaded a bevy of gyrating women wearing thong underwear and hotpants.

"Who in da 'hood tonight?" shouted Samuels, wearing a bathrobe and holding a bottle of Cristal as the limo door opened on one of western Illinois's densest sections of multifamily housing.

As a crowd quickly gathered, some exchanging high fives and hugs with the rich and famous local legend, Samuels explained his mission of charity.

"A lot of ballers make it out and forget where they came from. Not Rulon. Today is all about representin' the 618, staying true to my homies, and giving back—

juicy, heart-shaped back—to the hizzy."

With that, scantily-clad congenial young women paraded out of the limo and began mixing with the appreciative crowd. As he watched them bump and grind to the beat just blocks from the trash-strewn playground where he honed his jump shot,

Samuels grew misty-eyed.

"It's important to give back," he said, nodding toward the dancing women, his voice dropping to a whisper. "When I was a kid, we didn't have they fly fillies at home. Even in the clubs, the [collection of available females] was weak. It feels good to make a difference." ■

Where we spotlight those who talk about those who do

The following is an excerpt from NBC's Emmy-winning Olympic coverage.

Women's 200-Meter Butterfly, Finals

DAN HICKS: Hi. I'm Dan Hicks along with Rowdy Gaines. Welcome back to NBC's coverage of the Summer Olympic Games.

ROWDY GAINES: As we've seen through a series of heartwarming profiles, many of these fine athletes have overcome tremendous personal adversity for a chance at Olympic glory.

DAN: You betcha. The women's 200-meter butterfly is set to begin. If you're a sports fan, this event has everything you could want: a recovering gambling addict, two cancer survivors, and a mother of diabetic twins whose husband just lost his job. Don't touch that remote!

ROWDY: It's hard to pick a favorite here, Dan. The autistic prodigy who as a teenager had to wake up at 4:30 each morning to train in a polluted aqueduct, or the single mother who's half-blind.

DAN: Most of these competitors have spent their entire anguished lives preparing for the next two minutes.

ROWDY: Our swimmers are on their marks.

DAN: The Canadian favorite, Lacey Andrews, crouches in lane one. Despite losing her best friend to some snippy remarks two months ago, Andrews is coming off a personal best in the time trials, 2:06.51.

ROWDY: That's right. But she'll be hard-pressed to beat dyslexia sufferer and mail-fraud victim Suzy Berghoffen of Switzerland. She's gritty.

DAN: There's the gun, and they're off! And it's Brazil's Claudia Vilar in lane six with the early lead.

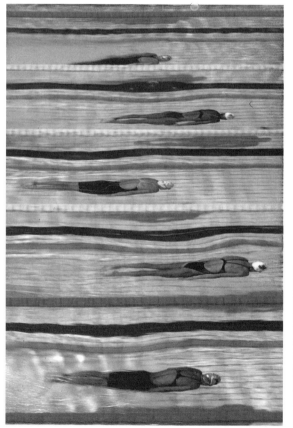

Adam Pretty/Getty Images Sport/Getty Images

Brother-with-Leukemia is really pouring it on in lane three.

What remarkable inner strength she has—no doubt from single-handedly managing her ailing father's sorghum farm.

ROWDY: She's being pushed hard by Scotland's Christine Fatheringham, in lane eight.

DAN: Oooh, Fatheringham's one to watch—she never knew her dad! Poor thing trained 'til the wee hours before coming home to an empty apartment while her mom worked a late-night janitorial shift. Can she make it all the way back?

ROWDY: We'll see! But here's the American Nancy Randall with a strong charge into the second turn. Look at that leg drive, spurred on by thoughts of her brother serving in Iraq.

And we're headed into the final lap. Here comes Ailing Father, she's trying to hold off Lost Best Friend, but OH MY, Brother-with-Leukemia is really pouring it on in lane three. BROTHER LEUKEMIA DOWN THE STRETCH! Speech Impediment drops back. Unemployed Husband is falling off. Sleep Apnea has nothing left!

AND BROTHER LEUKEMIA SLAPS THE WALL!

Childhood Eczema nabs the silver, Non-Hodgkin's Lymphoma the bronze.

Wow that was GREAT! Triumph over tragedy. Coming up: a latchkey kid, a man with a rare blood disorder, and a twice-divorced Cubs fan battle for Olympic glory in the discus. Keep it right here. ∎

WEB GEMS

We scour the web so you don't have to

Our pick for the best sports item available this month

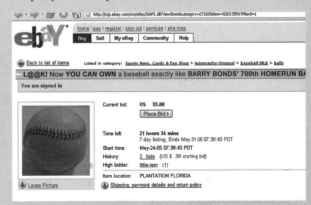

L@@K! NOW YOU CAN OWN A BASEBALL EXACTLY LIKE BARRY BONDS'S 700TH HOME-RUN BASEBALL!!!!

That's right, when Bonds hit his historic **700TH MAJOR LEAGUE HOME RUN** on September 17, 2004, play was stopped and the ball, worth hundreds of thousands of dollars, was retrieved and authenticated.

Now you can bid on the very similar ball, **NO RESERVE!!!** Make your bid, then find a secure, protective display case (this is one trophy you will want to show off!) Or else **PUT IT IN THE BANK.**

Right down to the white leather, red stitches, and stamped commissioner's autograph, it's official! Imagine your friends' disbelief when you show them a ball just like **BARRY BONDS'S FAMOUS 700th HOME-RUN BALL.**

BONDS'S HOME-RUN BALL is valued at **OVER $800,000. THINK WHAT YOU WOULD DO WITH THAT KIND OF MONEY!** Picture your wife's joy when you show her **THE HORSEHIDE-WRAPPED INVESTMENT OF A LIFETIME!** This ball is almost **IDENTICAL!!**

I could take this ball to an auction house like Sotheby's, but I am taking my chances by offering it here to quick thinkers like yourself.

Go ahead, bid securely—I accept PayPal or money orders. Buyer pays shipping.

Your big league dreams come true:

FANTASY BASEBALL FANTASY CAMP

January 23–29, Paramus, N.J.

EXPERIENCE THE LIFE OF A FANTASY BASEBALL PLAYER FOR A WHOLE WEEK!

Wonder what it's like for the best in the game? Now you can live it! At Fantasy Baseball Fantasy Camp you'll join a lineup of current and former fantasy stars like Paul C. Martin, Liz McCoy, Jeremy Belin, and Charlie Smucker as you compete for a $250 grand prize. Win or lose the tournament, your drafting strategy will get a much-needed makeover as you pick the brains of the very best make-believe GMs.

Fantasy Baseball Fantasy Camp is 24/7 fun. You'll spend your days at our linoleum-floored Fantasy Sports Complex—where the best roto players gather under the fluorescent lights to stir up trades and monitor hot stove news. You'll spend your evenings monitoring ESPN2 with fantasy icons like Fred Campe (the Skokie, Ind., electrician and famed "Roto Man" of the Web). Pull up your sleeping bag (not included) and glean valuable info as Campe reads aloud from *The Bill James Historical Baseball Abstract* and shares sabermetrics tips and memories from a career in fantasy baseball.

Beginners welcome! The level of your player-valuation skills does not matter. If you love the game of baseball as experienced through box scores and software analysis, you'll fit right in. So treat yourself. Or give the fantasy baseball fan in your life the gift of a lifetime.

Your Fantasy Baseball Fantasy Camp tuition includes:
- Special mock mock draft moderated by "Dr. Fantasy," Arnie Amler
- Your transactions and draft choices videotaped and analyzed by our expert staff
- Seminar: I Started Shane Halter over Miguel Tejada and Other Horror Stories
- Lunchtime sandwich (please specify ham or cheese) each day
- Uniform, cap, and calculator

CHOOSE FROM TWO GREAT PACKAGES!

The Fantasy Baseball Fantasy Camp package is $1,800.
For those campers who want to spend a little more time in Paramus, play indoor miniature golf, and schmooze with some of the assembled fantasy icons, we offer a limited number of VIP packages at $2,200.

The following are the personal notes of Stanley Frauenthal, inspector of workplace safety, U.S. Occupational Safety and Health Administration.

OSHA Inspection—NFL Training Camp

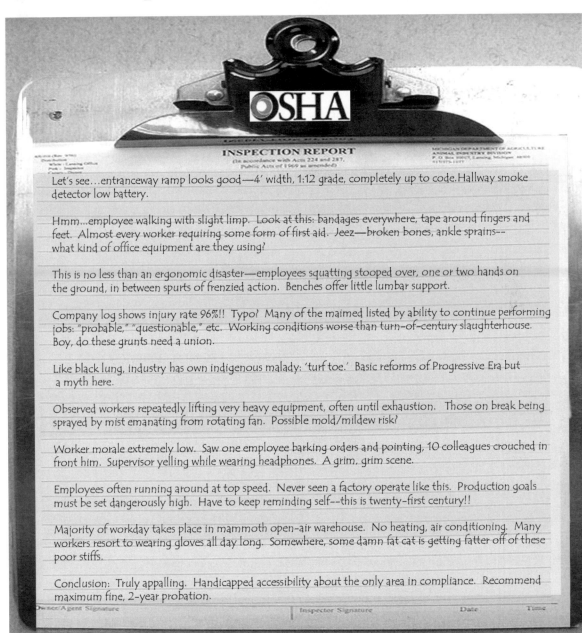

INSPECTION REPORT

Let's see…entranceway ramp looks good—4' width, 1:12 grade, completely up to code. Hallway smoke detector low battery.

Hmm…employee walking with slight limp. Look at this: bandages everywhere, tape around fingers and feet. Almost every worker requiring some form of first aid. Jeez—broken bones, ankle sprains--what kind of office equipment are they using?

This is no less than an ergonomic disaster—employees squatting stooped over, one or two hands on the ground, in between spurts of frenzied action. Benches offer little lumbar support.

Company log shows injury rate 96%!! Typo? Many of the maimed listed by ability to continue performing jobs: "probable," "questionable," etc. Working conditions worse than turn-of-century slaughterhouse. Boy, do these grunts need a union.

Like black lung, industry has own indigenous malady: 'turf toe.' Basic reforms of Progressive Era but a myth here.

Observed workers repeatedly lifting very heavy equipment, often until exhaustion. Those on break being sprayed by mist emanating from rotating fan. Possible mold/mildew risk?

Worker morale extremely low. Saw one employee barking orders and pointing, 10 colleagues crouched in front him. Supervisor yelling while wearing headphones. A grim, grim scene.

Employees often running around at top speed. Never seen a factory operate like this. Production goals must be set dangerously high. Have to keep reminding self--this is twenty-first century!!

Majority of workday takes place in mammoth open-air warehouse. No heating, air conditioning. Many workers resort to wearing gloves all day long. Somewhere, some damn fat cat is getting fatter off of these poor stiffs.

Conclusion: Truly appalling. Handicapped accessibility about the only area in compliance. Recommend maximum fine, 2-year probation.

Why I Stopped Boxing And Became A Writer

BY JOYCE CAROL OATES

My fascination with boxing is well known to many readers: I wrote a book on the subject, and a series of articles in the 1980s on the young champion Mike Tyson. But few if any know how I developed such a strong connection with the Sweet Science.

Certainly my father's love of the sport had a lot to do with it—I can still remember flipping through his copies of *The Ring* magazine as a young girl. Another catalyst was my first glimpse—while a graduate student at the University of Wisconsin—of the brash young Cassius Clay. But perhaps the most significant factor was getting the living shit knocked out of me when I stepped in the ring.

My career in pugilism began soon after receiving my master's from Wisconsin. Just 24, I felt strong pressure and expectations to pursue an academic career, but memories of those old copies of *The Ring* kept coming back to me, and I knew there was something else in store for me, something far beyond books.

Instinctively, I hit the gym and started bulking up. Weighing only 89 pounds at the time, I knew I had some major work to do. With the help of legendary trainer Nelson "Smelly" Giacomelli and a lot of raw eggs, within a year I was up to 117 pounds, and ready for my first fight in the bantamweight division.

As I looked across the ring at my opponent, Tony "Tomato" Talbot, I knew I had the edge. His eyes were bored, distracted—as if he were barely aware of me.

To him this fight was just something to do—a way to pass the time and earn a paycheck. But to me it was the very essence of being alive, indeed of fighting for one's life.

I remember thinking that here in the squared circle the enemy is not so much one's opponent as one's own intestinal fortitude. I remember thinking about being a young girl, about my father, but that's the last thing I remember because Talbot's first punch sent me flying into the fourth row.

I regained consciousness the following spring.

During my lengthy recovery I resolved that I would return to the ring, without my glasses.

My next bout, against Johnny "Pudding" Vogel, would prove similar to the Talbot fight, and ultimately the defining moment of my brief career in the ring.

As I would write years later in *On Boxing,* with my fight against Vogel very much in mind, "In a great fight, so much happens so swiftly and with such heart-stopping subtlety you cannot absorb it except to know that something profound is happening and it is happening in a place beyond words."

Many reviewers fawned over this passage, assuming that "a place beyond words" referred to the indescribable rapture of the sport. I was referring to being unable to speak as a result of my jaw being broken in six places. ■

Joyce Carol Oates has written over 100 books ranging from novels to poetry to nonfiction, including 1987's On Boxing.

Our recurring feature in which we revisit the sports lore of simpler times, via the *SMTM* archives

Lesbians For Liberty Inspire Imitators

Queers for the Buccaneers, Narcoleptics for the 'Niners also plan protests

Frustrated that their favorite WNBA team was ignoring its homosexual following, lesbian fans of the New York Liberty staged a protest "kiss-in" at an August 9 game, hugging and smooching during timeouts. Since the Lesbians for Liberty's much-publicized display, other neglected fan groups—from the Astros Albinos to Vegans for the Vikings—have sprung up to demand recognition.

One of the more outspoken of these new sports political action committees, or S-PACs, is the Phillies' Pheminists. Based in Langhorne, Pa., the Phems are led by retired hygienist Madeline Needleman, 57. Wearing an "I'm Pro-Choice and I VOTE for the All-Star Team" button, Needleman explained how the Phems were born:

"What the Liberty's fans did was very empowering. It forced me to reflect on the failed ratification of the ERA, and also the Phils' failure to sign a middle reliever with a respectable ERA."

Also inspired by the Lesbians is Tampa resident James Goldstein. Said Goldstein, "I love Florida football and I happen to be gay, which is pretty much the norm around here, although you won't hear [narrator] John Facenda say it in any NFL Films. Thousands of people like me root for the Bucs, yet the team's billboard ads and press guides don't even mention Stonewall. It's wrong." Goldstein created the Queers for the Buccaneers to encourage activism among like-minded fans. "Pride and pigskin," Goldstein explained, "That's the motto of the 'Neer-Queers."

Mergers between sports fan clubs and identity groups are not limited to political or sexual orientation. As Neil Heiss, founder of Doctors Without Borders or Raiders Tickets, explained, "As a physician, I often work late nights away from home at odd hours. Where are my box seats?"

"I've been asthmatic since junior high, libertarian since college, and I've always been fond of the Texas Rangers," said one female asking not to be named. "For years I couldn't find a group that matched those criteria and also loved *Waterworld*. Well, there are plenty of us! We'll be at tonight's game, and we're bringing a banner."

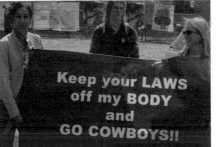

According to Tulane University sociologist Stephen J. Schmidt, the micro-Balkanization of sports fans is not new.

A member of the Church of Latter-Day and New Orleans Saints, he argues that identity politics and sports fandom stem from the same psychological impulse. "What does it mean to be a fan?" he asks. "Like political activism, rooting for a sports team carries the risk of failure, and makes one easy to marginalize. Supporting Ross Perot is no different from wearing a Cubs hat: It's a plea for a common humanity, a cry for connection. This is the very essence of sport, and of democratic society. A widespread merging of the two seems overdue."

Added Schmidt: "No matter where you fall on the political spectrum, it's hard to argue with the statement, 'We're here, we're queer, get a damn base hit.' " ■

VOLUME 100, NO. 10

SEPTEMBER

SPORTS MAGAZINE

THE MAGAZINE

BASEBALL STRIKE AVERTED

Players Win Right To Not Round Bases

Owners Acquiesce To Use Of "Ghost" Runners

Major League Baseball owners have averted a potentially disastrous strike by accepting the union's primary demand: that players no longer be forced to circle the bases after hitting the ball. According to the new rules, after putting a ball in play, the batter is free to seek medical attention or retire to the team clubhouse. The extent of each hit—single, double, triple, or home run—will be determined by umpire consensus. An imaginary, or "ghost," runner—a device often employed in backyard games and Wiffle Ball—will take his place on the base paths, and the batter will remain in the lineup.

Spearheaded by representatives of the San Francisco Giants slugger, the so-called Barry Bonds Rule won 11th-hour acceptance when commissioner Bud Selig convinced team owners they could realize millions of dollars in savings via imaginary employees.

"This was a difficult decision, but it's in the best interests of the game," explained Selig. "Too many

Bases loaded under baseball's new rules

ballplayers have been getting hurt on the base paths, forcing franchises to spend unnecessary millions on marginally talented, completely unmarketable pinch runners. The Devil Rays, for example, lost 114 workdays to base-path injuries last year. Without imaginary stand-ins, how can they compete? And the fans, they want to see a major star like Barry at the plate, not in the trainer's room."

Bonds's spokesperson was not speaking to the press, but his spokesperson's spokesperson explained that the Giants left fielder was "most likely pleased," as Bonds had grown weary of ritually circling the bases.

"After slamming a homer, a player should be rewarded, not assigned busywork," said the spokesperson. "Why make some-

one of Barry's stature dance for his pay? We know the run counts. Just step on home plate, and put it in the books. Barry's had to shuck 'n' jive for the crowd *over 700 times.* It's humiliating—he's not Stepin Fetchit. And those 360-foot journeys add up on the legs. After his three-homer night against the Braves in June, Barry's hike from the postgame buffet to the [Cadillac] Escalade was as painful as sitting through that [*Divine Secrets of the*] *Ya-Ya Sisterhood* movie."

The use of ghost runners will begin immediately. In the case of more than one phantom runner safely reaching base, each will proceed sequentially toward home plate via use of "force," another homespun convention long enjoyed by rural and unpopular children. ∎

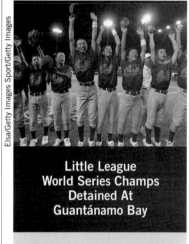

NEWS IN BRIEF

Little League World Series Champs Detained At Guantánamo Bay

Phillies Fans Boo Eagles Fans' Booing Attempt

Switch-Hitting Switch Hitter Hit By Pitch, Switch

ESPN The Fragrance Now Available

CORRECTIONS

In our article "Scoring Blitz in Major League Soccer," we misstated the score of the D.C. United/Columbus Crew game. It was not 8–5; it was 0–0.

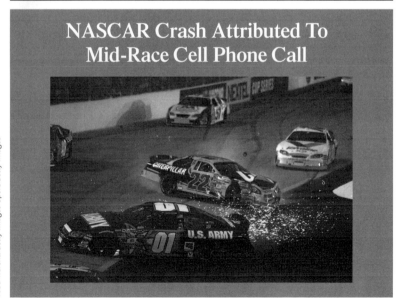

NASCAR Crash Attributed To Mid-Race Cell Phone Call

All-Luxury-Box Stadium Pretty Quiet On Game Day

Despite rave reviews and a sold-out season, the Arizona Cardinals' new $650 million corporate-suites-only football stadium is drawing criticism from players for its lack of atmosphere.

"It's nice, but it's kind of like being at an aquarium," said linebacker Ryan Perkins, after his team's 24–13 home loss to the Packers. "All the fans are behind thick glass, nibbling on snacks. You just don't get that 'madhouse' feel like at Lambeau."

"I'm glad corporate ticket sales built this place— our locker room is beautiful," said fullback Eddie Ludman. "And I don't miss hearing the boobirds. But jeez, it's church-quiet out there. Right after [receiver Deion] McBride caught that TD bomb, all we heard was the ref drawing a breath, before blowing his whistle."

"It's kind of like being in an aquarium."

Safety D'Shaun Shigley also finds the quietude dispiriting: "Lack of fan support is one thing, but I can't even tell if people are at the game or not—all the windows are tinted."

Receiver Frits Armarty let a key third-down pass slip through his fingertips in the fourth quarter and appeared perplexed after the game. Said the receiver: "I was hearing footsteps all day out there, man. I gotta get me some quieter cleats."

Cardinals officials have addressed the lack of atmosphere, with limited success.

Says Fan Experience Coordinator Ian Plotkin, "We tried to build a Dawg Pound kind of culture in our Club Level, called the Bird House. We handed out birdseed for the fans and tried to initiate mass birdcalls when our defense was on the field. But the suites are soundproof, so it was tough to pull off.

Nobody could see or hear each other unless they were in the same suite. So we ended up just giving away the bird feed, as a promotional tie-in with Petco.

"We thought about removing the glass altogether, to create more of a sense of shared experience, but some companies felt that if cheering football fans were audible over their teleconferencing equipment, it would hamper productivity."

Coach Dennis Green has tried to make the best of a difficult situation. "I don't miss wearing that bulky headset around the sideline, no sir," said Green. "With the fans behind glass, if I have a question for Clancy Pendergast [defensive coordinator], I just cup my hands like this and call to him up in the booth,

'Hey—Clancy!' So there's some upside to the silence."

Earlier in the season CBS added full-time background music, like that played on highlight shows. With 35 seconds between plays, it tended to drone. Said producer Barry Ignall, "Hard-charging symphonies just didn't feel right for watching players shuffle on and off the field, and referees conferring about the spot." The experiment was halted after one week. Networks have resorted to piping in canned crowd noise for home viewers.

"In a way," added Plotkin, "we're kind of glad our players can't see inside the suites. Most of the time fans are milling around, backs to the field, ordering apple-tinis and discussing interest rates." ∎

Texas Ranked #1 By J.D. Power & Associates

#2 Toyota Camry, #3 USC

Just one week into the season, college football's complex rankings system received yet another wrinkle when J. D. Power and Associates announced its annual quality survey results.

The marketing firm's findings augment those already in use by the elaborate Bowl Championship Series (which includes polls conducted by, among others, Harris Interactive, *USA Today,* the Associated Press, the *New York Times,* Scripps Howard News Service, ESPN, Zagat's, and the Sierra Club). A list of the most influential rankings systems, and their results, is at right.

Final College Football Rankings			
System	#1	#2	#3
HarrisInteractive	Texas	USC	Penn State
USA TODAY ESPN TOP25 COACHES' POLL	Texas	USC	Penn State
J.D. POWER AND ASSOCIATES	Texas	Toyota Camry	USC
Consumer Reports	Maytag #MDG7500A	USC	Red Roof Inn
People	Texas	Ben Affleck	Oklahoma
LEONARD MALTIN'S MOVIE & VIDEO GUIDE	It's A Wonderful Life	USC	Oklahoma!

NBA: No More Non-Dunks

Outside-shooting ban to make league more fan-friendly

NBA officials announced that the league would no longer award points for shots taken without physically jamming the ball into the net.

"What brings fans to their feet?" asked league spokesman Andrew Grifo, "Free throws? I don't think so. What hot game highlights does ESPN show? Crisp bounce passes? Unselfish ball movement culminating in a 12-foot bank shot? It's dunks. Focus group after focus group says fans love dunks. We simply want to encourage more of what they want to see: 360-degree, alley-oop, behind the back, in-your-face reverse phi slamma tomahawk jammas."

Along with three-pointers and jump shots, lay-ups will also no longer count.

Along with three-pointers and jump shots, lay-ups will also no longer count. In case of a foul, the player will be allowed a pair of dunks attempted from four feet out. If the player was in the act of dunking when the foul occurred, the dunk will count, and the player will be allowed an additional "free dunk" attempt from anywhere in the paint.

"Scoring might be down for a few months," said Commissioner David Stern, "as teams adjust to ramping up their throw-downs, but in the long run,

when you factor in video game sales, this is nothing but a plus.

"We are still determining whether to award extra points depending on degree of difficulty and artistry, as determined by the head referee.

"Personally," added Stern, "I think this is a return to the game's peach basket roots. Three-pointers, set shots, pull-ups, screened jumpers—all of these detract from basketball's purest essence: the stuffing of ball through hoop." ■

Joe Murphy/NBA/Getty Images

Here's What's Unique About Baseball

BY BILL TATUM

I know there are a lot of great sports out there. Thrilling spectacles, intense competition, remarkable athleticism. But it's impossible to deny that baseball, our national pastime, is unique.

For starters, there's the absence of a clock. In a world that grows ever more hurried and frantic by the day, we can always look to baseball for that serene, timeless feel. There are no timeouts; there's no fouling your opponent to send him to the free-throw line, or taking a knee to run out the clock. You simply play the game until your team has exhausted its allotment of chances.

But despite this leisurely pace, the game remains thrilling, gripping, suspenseful. As I've said to my TV audience so many times over the years: What makes baseball so exciting is that, ultimately, it's a game of inches. Nearly every pitch, in fact, is not just a matter of inches but a matter of fractions-of-inches.

But I think what really sets baseball apart—and you'll hear my colleagues in the booth say this all the time—is that you just never know when you're going to see something on the field that you've never seen in your life. It happens time and time again: Even an old-timer like me, who thinks he's seen it all, will witness some implausible turn of events, some absurd base-running blunder, some bizarre play that has us scrambling for our rule books. It is moments like these that I cherish, because it reminds me what is so wonderful and unique about this game I love. ■

The author has been the color analyst for Chicago White Sox games for 53 years.

Everything That Guy Says Is True Of All Sports

BY ALEXANDER MORROW

Is that guy senile or drunk or both? Yeah, all other sports have clocks. Really? This guy ever seen tennis? Golf? Volleyball? Bowling?

As for baseball being a game of inches, I'm wondering what sport *isn't* determined by inches? I mean, have you ever shot a basketball? If you're off by an inch or two, it ain't going in. And I've watched hockey all my life: Virtually every shot on goal is either saved or missed by about an inch. And I'm not even getting into track and field.

What's more—while some plays in baseball are certainly determined by inches, I could swear baseball is also the only sport where, rather than aiming for a precise, small target or goal, you're actually trying to smack the ball into the 30th row of the stands. Sort of weakens the whole "game of inches" thing, doesn't it?

As for baseball's unique ability to provide moments that even a lifelong sports fan has never seen, I have seven words: "The band is out on the field!" ■

The author is a sales clerk and sports fan.

Controversial Baseball Memoirs

The scandalous tell-all baseball confessional is a time-honored tradition, from Jim Bouton's legendary Ball Four *(1970) to seminal diaries like Ebenezer Duckworth's* Peanuts, Crackerjack, and Polio: My Life Whilst in the Seasonal Employ of the Toledo Professional Base-Ball Club *(1911). More recently, David Wells, in his 2003 autobiography,* Perfect I'm Not! Boomer on Beer, Brawls, Backaches and Baseball, *claimed he pitched his perfect game while he was "still half drunk" from the previous night, and he estimated that 25 to 40 percent of Major League players used steroids. Jose Canseco's infamous memoir* Juiced *(2005) supported this claim. Here is a look at some of the most infamous revelations made in baseball autobiographies.*

One of the earliest accounts of the burgeoning national pastime, Birchley Titcomb's *Peccadilloes, Imbroglios, and Spittle: My Life as the Pitcher for the Louisville Colonels* (1893), was banned in schools.

"It was raining the blood of the innocent."

CHAPTER THE FOURTH
"In my best and most Christian estimation, between one quarter and two fifths of all professional base-ball players have used and in many cases abused performance-enhancing 'bar-bells,' the long-term effects of which are not yet known. . . . Said bar-bells are easy to procure, and it is as apparent as the nose upon one's face that they alter the game in grotesque ways.

One of the 'hopped-up' ball-players, T. S. McGillicutty of the Rochester Nine, hit three home-runs in but a single month."

Ruth: Photo File/Major League Baseball/Getty Images

No baseball life is filled with as much legend and lore as Babe Ruth's. His autobiography, *From the Mouth of Babe* (1946), was both praised and denounced for its frank, "warts and all" portrayal of the icon:

"If there's one thing that I get asked more than anything else, it's about that 1932 World Series: did I or didn't I 'call' my home run off of [Charlie] Root by pointing to the centerfield stands? Well, the fact of the matter is, I sure did. And what's more, having caroused and carried on with the fellas the night before, I was still half-naked."

And fans will forever talk of the revelations made by former Pirate pitcher Dock Ellis in his 1976 autobiography *Dock Ellis in the Country of Baseball,* namely that he pitched a no-hitter after ingesting three tabs of acid:

"On June 12, 1970, I pitched a no-hitter despite the fact that the game-time temperature was 136 degrees, it was raining the blood of the innocent, and I was a half-full glass of orange juice. People still make a fuss about that to this day, but the fact remains, if you're responsible and experienced, and you know what you're doing, you can excel if you're a glass of juice, a centaur, just about anything. One time, Keith Hernandez went 3-for-4 off of me on a day that he was Joan of Arc." ■

LOST & FOUND

Our correspondents are always on the lookout for noteworthy sports artifacts *Athletic success can bring great wealth but requires expensive upkeep. Here's a candid look at one anonymous pro's monthly bills.*

General Ledger (Accounts Payable) ▓▓▓▓▓▓ (Pro Athlete)

operty	Date	Period	Debit	Credit	Description	B
)80	01/14	1	$2,509		Stretch Coach	
)80	01/16	1	$2,738		Personal Sous-Chef	
)80	01/16	1	$3,325		Chef Stretcher	
)80	01/20	1	$3,780		Bodyguard for body double	
)80	01/22	1	$4,763		Posse rental	
)80	01/22	1	$2,100		Receptionist for cell phone	
)80	01/24	1	$1,700		Scrivener	
)80	01/30	1	$4,505		Bling Leader	

POLL RESULTS

Which Was the Worst Cheating Incident in Modern Baseball History?

• *1975: Gaylord Perry lip-synchs National Anthem.* (36%)

• *1994: Albert Belle celebrates home run by decanting Merlot from corked bat.* (27%)

• *2004: Texas Rangers awarded contract to rebuild Iraq.* (37%)

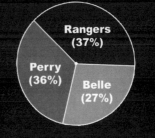

Rangers (37%)
Perry (36%)
Belle (27%)

Legendary broadcaster Jim Stodges, 86, retired this month after 62 years in the booth. Below is his final half-inning, with rookie play-by-play man Scott "Raise the Roof" Long.

Jim Stodges, Hall Of Fame Broadcaster—Final Inning

SCOTT: So we go to the bottom of the ninth. New York needs two runs to tie, three to win. Here's the pitch, Ackerman swings, hits it in the air down the right-field line, Shaw gets there . . . but he can't make the play! He got there in time, but he dropped it like Brad dropped Jennifer. His third error in four games. Oooh, that's gotta hurt. Gimme an "E"!

Jim Stodges

JIM: The "cranks," or "fans," who populate the right-field bleacher-seats are giving him quite a razzing. "Highball Shaw" some of the wags have dubbed him, after his preference not only in pitches to sock but in postgame refreshments as well.

SCOTT: That's right, old-timer. Shaw and his agent just finalized the terms on a new three-year deal. With incentives he could make up to $5.65 million a year. Wouldn't mind some of THAT suga' sprinkled on Daddy's pancakes!

JIM: And like many of his fellow Kentuckians, or "Goldenrods," he no doubt spends his off-seasons mining bituminous coal from dawn 'til dusk.

SCOTT: Probably! So Randy Ackerman is standing on second. Stan Moses on the mound, looking in at the next batter, Duke Shalen, who is an absolute STUD. He's got THIRTY-FOUR Johnsons this year—for a rookie, that is just SIIICK! And listen to what the PA cranks when he walks to the plate: "Big Poppa"—the Notorious B.I.G., baby! Much love, Biggie. Respect!

JIM: Shalen is a strapping young quadroon who can hit the ball a Texas mile in a New York minute. He

Scott Long

has a square jaw, a firm handshake, and a reputed weakness for toffee.

SCOTT: Here's the pitch, swung on, hit deep to right . . . Forget about it, BAY-BEE! [*singing*] Ding-Dong, the pitch is dead! That's Shalen's 35th Jimmy-Jack of the year, and it ties this game at five in the ninth inning! The fans are going BANANAS! [*singing*] I love it when you call me Big Poppa!

JIM: Ah, Dame Fortune is a fickle mistress. The visiting Chicago nine seemed to have secured the ballgame with their "rally" in the eighth inning. In said frame, 30 Windy City toes danced the Charleston across home-plate, a result of the club's time-tested "a base-hit slap, a stolen-base thunderclap, and a base-on-balls for lagniappe" brand of ball-play. But now the New York nonet has settled the balance with that monster of modernity, the "long-ball."

SCOTT: And look who's coming up to bat now. Boom-shaka-laka! It's big, bad Kyle Terrowski, who's got 32 Johnsons and almost as many tattoos. Bro, ya

Scott: I love it when you call me Big Poppa! Jim: Ah, Dame Fortune is a fickle mistress.

DON'T wanna mess with this dude. The PA is blasting Creed, and the fans want to see some rock 'n' roll from Terrowski, they want to see another money shot. First pitch low, ball one.

JIM: Can the burly Pole duplicate the feat of his predecessor in the lineup, that being young, toothsome Mister Shalen? Can he thrill the "cranks" by delivering yet another cork-and-hide parcel to their peanut-shell-littered domain?

SCOTT: There's a called strike, the count is one-and-one. Terrowski steps out of the batter's box. That pitch was brought to you by Grey Goose—The World's Best Tasting Vodka. Terrowski steps back in. Moses deals . . . that ball is swung on, hit pretty deep to left, Snow going back, at the wall, looking up . . . THAT IS SOOOO NOT COMING BACK! GOODBYE, GET LOST, NO WE CAN'T BE FRIENDS.

JIM: Magnificent! Simply magnificent! A splendid conclusion to a valiant battle. One can do naught but stand in one's place and respectfully applaud these bat-and-ball warriors.

SCOTT: [*singing, dancing*] I like to move it move it, I like to move it move it . . . !

JIM: What drama! What glorious theater! Oh, this grand national pastime of baseball: Will she ever be challenged as our fair nation's most belov'd spectacle?

SCOTT: For Jim Stodges, I'm Scott Long saying: This is how we roll. ∎

Yogi To Press: "I Ain't No Novelty"

"Stop with the damn caricature"

Yogi Berra, Hall of Fame catcher and beloved malaprop geyser, has declared he will no longer provide funny "Yogi-isms" to reporters.

"Look, I don't mind talkin' baseball," said the famously affable Yankee legend. "But these kids call me up trying to wring some wise new folk saying or cutesy sound bite outta me for tomorrow's column, and it gets old. I don't care if you're on deadline, I'm not some ball-playing Yoda. I can speak in complete sentences."

Appearing grizzled and half-shaven, the usually charming Berra stood stone-faced behind his dark tinted glasses as he addressed the media. "How would you like it if every time the sun set, some wet-behind-the-ears newsy came up and asked, 'Hey Yogi, if it gets late early out here, what happens during day-

> "It ain't the heat," said Yogi of his constant hounding by the press, "it's the humility. These guys have none."

light savings? Eh? Eh?' Like I'm some kind of vending machine for beat reporters. Make up your own damn aphorisms."

"It ain't the heat," said Yogi of his constant hounding by the press, "it's the humility. These guys have none. They follow me around with their notebooks, just begging me to mangle some syntax, so they can file another 'Let's all laugh at old Yogi' column. Let me tell you something: The dumb-guy schtick was fun for a while—I know it landed me those Miller Lite spots back in the '80s—but no more. Enough is enough. My life ain't a minstrel show. You wanna talk? Let's talk about the issues: Iraq. Universal health care. Ask me if I've read any good books lately. Let's have a *conversation*."

Before departing, Berra added that his decision was indeed final: "I know I said, 'It ain't over 'til it's over,' but as far as me playin' talking bobblehead to these son of a guns, it's over." ∎

Since When Can An Announcer Get Fired For On-Air Hate Speech?

BY J. B. GALISHAW

It's a sign of the times: An announcer just can't get away with saying anything controversial anymore. I grew up listening to guys like Harry Caray and Ralph Kiner, who would call it as they saw it. If a player messed up, they'd say it. If they were drunk on the air, you could tell. If they salted their broadcasts with ethnic slurs, it would get overlooked.

But these days all of that is disappearing. Just as corporations have bought all the old stadium names, business interests have bought the very soul of the enterprise. If an announcer says something audacious, a few prude grannies call up the team to complain, and the team, fearing a pullout from their sponsors, immediately gives the guy the ax after 30 years. It was hardly a shock, then, that the latest casualty was the Kansas City Royals' legendary color man, Larry "Bleep" LaRocca.

He was known for being as unprepared as he was outspoken.

Bleep was from the old school: Having come up in the 1950s, long before the information age, he was known for being as unprepared as he was outspoken. The opposing pitcher was simply "that guy" or, as the situation warranted, "that ugly guy."

And where younger colleagues would get bogged down in details—reciting every statistic that produc-

ers fed them—LaRocca would paint the games with broad brushstrokes, saying "We're in the middle innings" to indicate anything between the third and eighth; "We're tied" to mean a one-run game; and referring to all Latin players as "Pancho."

But these days there's not much room for a broadcaster who's as willing to speak his mind as LaRocca, and last month the Royals released him after he referred to the team's 14–3 drubbing of the Indians as "a latter-day Wounded Knee."

LaRocca's firing is just another sad example of the continuing erosion of our First Amendment rights. You can't check out any books on building fertilizer bombs without the government finding out, and you can't mention the name and address of your former mistress in the course of describing a routine ground ball.

But what I'll miss most are LaRocca's inimitable catchphrases. After an unusual play, he would always make it even more memorable with a trademark expression of surprise. Where a less creative announcer would opt for something safe like "Holy Toledo, a triple play!" LaRocca was known for such folksy, homespun sayings as "A triple play? Well shit on my face and call me a two-dollar hooker."

J. B. Galishaw *is our senior editor and the author of* Seven Words You CAN Say on Television.

Our recurring feature in which we revisit the sports lore of simpler times, via the *SMTM* archives

U.S. Men's Olympic Basketball Team Eyeing 1972 Silver Medals

Thirty-two years ago the U.S. men's basketball team lost the gold-medal game to the Soviets due to questionable officiating, and refused to claim their silver medals. To this day, those medals lie unclaimed in a vault in Switzerland.

Said Team USA cocaptain Allen Iverson, "So we could get those, or what?"

Despite losses to the unheralded squads of Puerto Rico, Lithuania, and Argentina—resulting in a disappointing bronze-medal finish—the U.S. team's hunger for shinier Olympic hardware has not faded.

"If it's a money issue, we want to make it clear that's not a problem," remarked Team USA member Amare Stoudemire, "I'm prepared to pay whatever it takes to floss some Olympic chrome."

Team USA learned of the 1972 scandal from a documentary shown to all visiting athletes upon their arrival at the Olympic Village. At the time, team members failed to see any connection between the historic controversy and their own plight; but as the days went by, the relevance became clear.

"During the screening I would glance up now and then from my GameBoy," said USA forward Shawn Marion, "and I'd wonder, 'Why are we getting this lesson in ancient history?'"

Many on the team agreed that the movie initially failed to resonate. Said guard LeBron James, "Sure, we could feel for them getting a bad call . . . but everyone gets bad calls. We get bad calls all the time."

Yet after Team USA's listless loss to Argentina, Marion had an epiphany: "Those silver medals are just sitting there!"

"It just seemed silly for these '72 guys to remain so worked up about it," said USA forward Richard Jefferson, "I mean, the Cold War is over, right?"

After a team meeting, the '04 squad agreed to offer the 1972 team their new bronze medals in exchange for the '72 silvers.

"The only reason the '72 team rejected their medals was they thought they were tainted," explained co-captain Tim Duncan, "but there's nothing tainted about these bronzes."

Duncan then summarized his team's message to their 1972 antecedents: "Little help?" ■

Chris McGrath/Getty Images Sports/ Getty Images

THIS MONTH IN HISTORY

September 1, 1964
At Beatles' first-ever San Francisco concert, John Lennon tells adoring crowd: "We're bigger than Jesus Alou."

September 12, 2001
By presidential decree, "God Bless America" to be sung before all games of tag and duck duck goose.

VOLUME 100, NO. 11

OCTOBER

SPORTS MAGAZINE

THE MAGAZINE

PERCENTAGE OF ATHLETES WHO GIVE 110% DROPS TO 119%

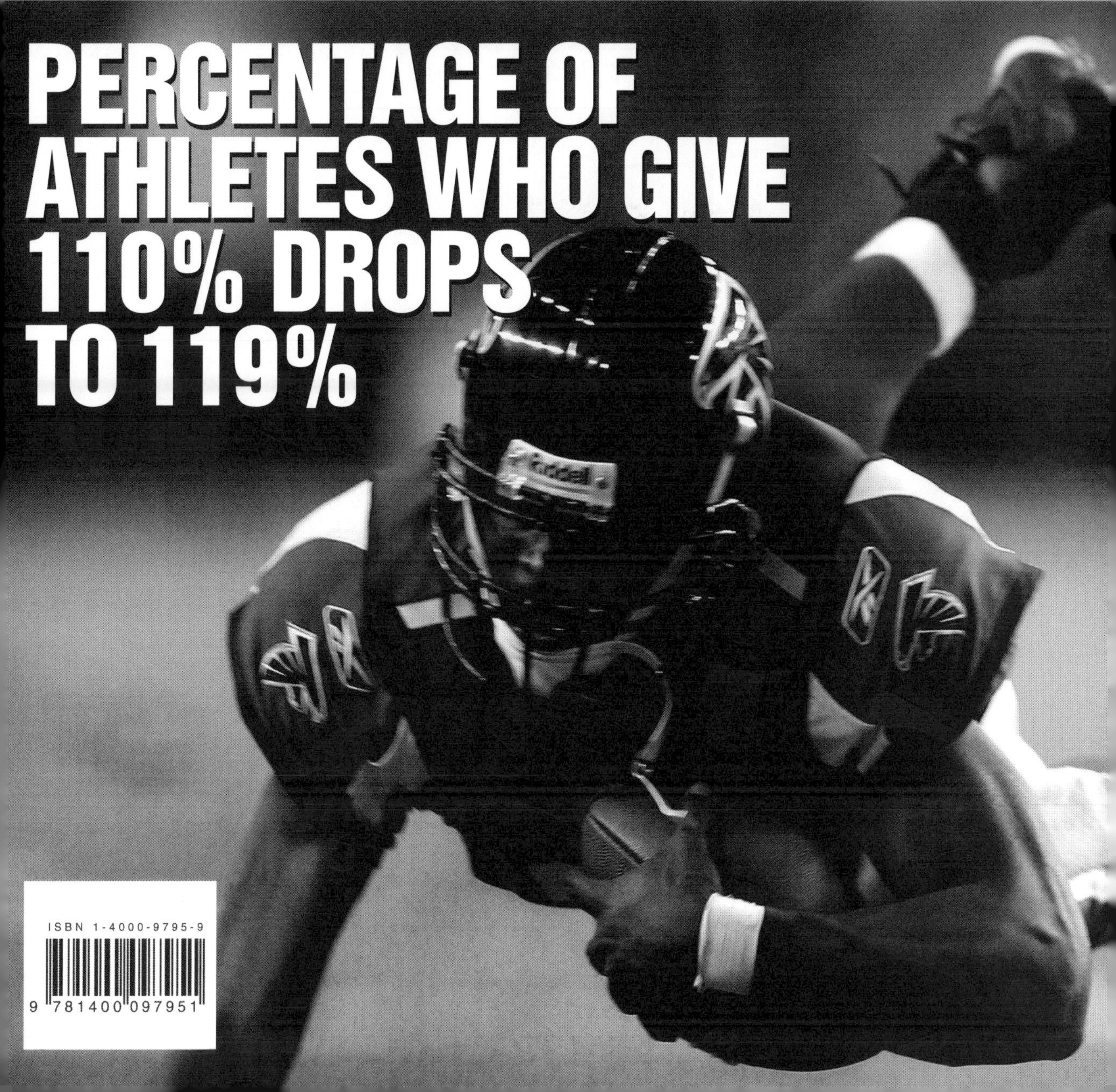

ISBN 1-4000-9795-9

9 781400 097951

Fire In Belly Nearly Extinguished

Researchers at Emory University have discovered that the percentage of pro athletes who give 110 percent has been declining for years, from an all-time high of 160 percent in the mid-1970s to a mere 119 percent today.

The triple-blind study also found that the percentage of athletes who take it to the next level—nearly 130 percent 20 years ago—is now at a lowly 106 percent. Said research director Eugene Fielding, 41, "Most of us grew up watching athletes who gave 110 to 150 percent—from Dick Butkus and Bobby Hull in my father's generation to Lawrence Taylor and

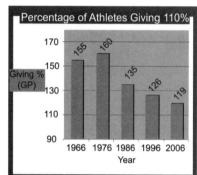

Michael Jordan in my own. But within a decade, competitors who give 110 percent or more will represent less than 101 percent of all professional athletes."

Admittedly, the margin for error (±100%) is high. But, as Fielding explains, not as high as it once was: "Methods of measuring GP [giving percentage] were extremely primitive for many years—it was based largely on grass stains."

In 1993 this was rectified when scientists determined that broadcasters' postgame analysis is a far more accurate indicator.

The findings confirm what is known as the Theory of Don't Make 'Em Like They Used To, as voiced by 200 percent of TV analysts and uncles. ■

NCAA Basketball Switches To All-Tournament Schedule

Demented December, Frantic February to make March less mad

The NCAA has announced that it will repeat its popular Division I basketball tournament, commonly known as March Madness, several times throughout the year.

"It's a successful model," said NCAA spokesperson Julia Warren, "so why confine it to a single month?"

In essence, the plan substitutes the regular season with eight consecutive 64-team tournaments. After a winner is crowned and celebrated, the next month brings a brand-new bracket.

Said Warren, "If you love March Madness, you're going to love Frantic February just as much. It's better actually, because it comes earlier.

"The new basketball calendar starts with Screw-

Nathaniel S. Butler/NBA/Getty Images

ball September—where you have no idea who's coming out of the preseason hot. Anyone can make the Final Four before the leaves fall. Then comes Off The Wall October, chock-full of spooky upsets. And get your office pool ready, because the day after Halloween it's Nutso November."

According to the NCAA, the grueling schedule will improve the quality of play.

"You're going to see a more honest, accurate brand of basketball," said NCAA president Myles Brand. "Any tourney squad can get lucky in March—Villanova in '85 comes to mind—but could Rollie Massimino's plucky band of scrappers have defeated mighty Georgetown again, in Madcap May?

"We will never know . . . but now we will know, should it happen again—because under the new schedule, hours after being feted at the White House 'Nova would be tipping off against 16-seed Purdue in the opening round of Apeshit April." ■

Hot New Video Game Lets You Control Characters Playing Video Games

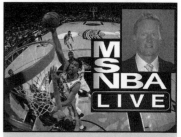

Belichick Accused Of Illegally Enhancing Own Cognition

Super Bowl legacy at risk from gene therapy charges

Bill Belichick's former college English professor has accused the Patriots' head coach of experimenting with cognition-enhancing gene therapy. "I had Bill in an English course in '75, the Literature of Oppression," said Donald Kerman, English Department co-chair at Wesleyan University. "By the time most students had turned in essays examining the writings of Du Bois and Solzhenitsyn, Bill was still struggling to learn to type. No way a guy like that masterminds three championships without a few think-drinks."

While rumors of Belichick's alleged visits to the Biogen laboratories in Cambridge, Mass., have swirled for years, until now no one had formally accused the coach of illegally increasing his neurological capacity.

Kerman produced several papers allegedly written by Belichick when the coach was a college student. Although coherent, they were unfocused, ill-structured, and ranged in grade from D to B-. Asked Kerman, "Does this look like the work of a man who

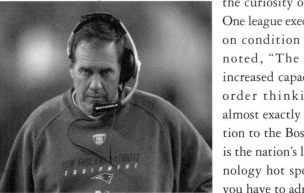

would go on to create and implement groundbreaking defenses—complete with audibles and line stunts—on a weekly basis?"

Given Belichick's spotty head coaching success before coming to the Patriots, his transformation into the biggest brain in the sport has long piqued the curiosity of NFL officials. One league executive, speaking on condition of anonymity, noted, "The timing of his increased capacity for higher-order thinking coincides almost exactly with his relocation to the Boston area, which is the nation's leading biotechnology hot spot. It's curious, you have to admit."

Adding to the suspicions, a bottle of ginseng tablets was famously photographed on Belichick's desk by an AP reporter. At the time, however, such memory-enhancing drugs were not on the NFL's illegal substance list.

The most recent charges have encouraged others in the game to speak up. Said Philadelphia head coach Andy Reid: "It's like *Flowers for Algernon* with that guy. He loses 56 games in his first six years.

Jim Isaac/Getty Images Sport/Getty Images

The Browns—the woeful Cleveland Browns—run him out of town. Since then, poof, three [Super Bowl] rings. The worst part of it is the implication for our nation's children—they're so impressionable."

The impact in schools remains to be seen. According to some education officials, math and debate clubs are the most at risk. Says National Education Association spokesperson Betsy Lichtig, "Soon we'll see some poor 12-year-old kid toying with his very genetic code just so he can come up with a decent rebuttal about global warming." ∎

Offensive Line Coach Constantly Shouting Offensive Lines

". . . crush them in my hand, eat one, and mail the other to your crippled granny, ref!"

"BLOCK, you sissy-pissing banana-faggots!"

Ignoring trends in both education and society at large, Rockville (MD) High School assistant football coach Bob Pilson continues to motivate his players with brutal, oft-bewildering verbal assaults. Barking commands laced with homophobia, xenophobia, misogyny, self-loathing, a Kipling-era admiration of social Darwinism, and the occasional coaching tip, Pilson has helped lead the Tigers to a 2–5 record.

"I was late picking up a blitzer in the second quarter against Bloomsburg," explained left guard Zach DaRusso. "Before the whistle had even blown, I heard The Pill [Coach Pilson] yelling, 'CHRIST ON A CRAP-STICK, DARUSSO! YOU MOVE SLOWER THAN A RETARD IN A VOTING BOOTH. THIS MUST BE WHY THE WOP-SLOP AT YOUR FAMILY'S PIZZA JOINT IS ALWAYS SERVED COLD!'

"I was, like, 'Huh?' My dad's an accountant." ∎

"If our troops had had this line's spineless attitude during The Big One, your mommas would be getting butt-boinked by Nips right now!"

NBA Rookie Apologizes For Future Behavior

Pre-emptive mea culpa covers "all indiscretions to come"

Steve Nassau, the highly touted Denver Nuggets rookie, issued a blanket apology today for any and all future run-ins with the law.

"This is a difficult day for me," said an emotional Nassau, reading from a prepared statement, "but I know the sooner I say 'I'm sorry,' the better. I don't want to wait and wait until, next thing you know, I commit some felony. And it gets blown all out of proportion by the media.

"So, I would like to apologize to many people—my loved ones, the fans, and my current and future teammates on the Nuggets, and elsewhere. There's no other way to put this: What I am going to do was wrong."

Basketball insiders say the 19-year-old shooting guard, who joined the NBA straight from high school earlier this year, was headed for a promising career until his dark future caught up with him.

The open-ended apology includes—but is not limited to—such misbehavior as substance and spousal abuse, choking a superior, gunplay, spitting or

urinating on fans, and betting on the Cincinnati Reds.

"I'd also like to apologize to some people rarely recognized. Like the janitor in a Houston strip club, forced to sweep up broken glass at 3 A.M. a few years from now, when I'll most likely throw a drunken heckler through a window."

To show his commitment, Nassau announced he would set aside a percentage of his three-year, $7 million contract to support future illegitimate offspring.

"I want to say today that all my support and love will always go to the children I will one day mistakenly conceive."

"It was a great speech," remarked ESPN analyst Tony Kornheiser midway through Nassau's apology. "Steve was a real man up there. Now, when I learn he's groped a team employee, or perhaps punched out a cotton candy vendor, I don't have to wait an entire news cycle to hear an apology."

Nassau concluded: "I obviously have regrets about all these things I'm probably going to do, but I just hope I can move on. What's in the future is in the future." ■

> ## "All my support and love will always go to the children I will one day mistakenly conceive."

Latest Polls Reveal America's Favorite Sport Is Polling

A ccording to the latest Gallup and Newsweek/MSNBC polls, Americans prefer polling to any other sport or activity.

Says CNN pollster Jeremy Putzel, "Sports surveys used to attract only the lonely and the congenitally opinionated, but in recent years almost any sports poll—no matter how trivial—garners a robust response. Should the Chargers fire their special teams coach? Who will be leading at halftime of the NBA All-Star Game, East or West? Nearly the entire world has an opinion."

Measured by Internet traffic and radio call-in show phone logs, the very act of querying the public—an undertaking once reserved for determining political and cola preferences—has blossomed into the national pastime.

Madison, Wis., teenager Morton Hickey explains the appeal of instant polling: "I like watching baseball, but Tony LaRussa doesn't exactly ask me who I'd rather bring in from the pen, Randy Flores or Ricardo Rincon. ESPN.com does. It's a more fulfilling relationship."

Adds Hickey's neighbor Jimmy Livingston, "Watching the game takes three hours. Giving my opinion on the game takes ten seconds. Seems pretty clear which way to go."

Last month a CNN/SI.com

> **"Watching the game takes three hours. Giving my opinion on the game takes ten seconds. Seems pretty clear which way to go."**

poll that asked, "What will you watch tonight?" garnered an astounding 356,556 votes.

"I don't remember what I ended up watching," says participant and avid e-pollster Ari Balloo. "It might have been an episode of *Everybody Loves Raymond,* but I will tell you that I stayed up until the polls closed, and Jazz-Timberwolves was the winner."

"The Grady Little thing, that was really a watershed poll," remembers baseball fan Sam Altman about a CBS SportsLine poll initiated three minutes after the end of Game 7 of the 2003 ALCS. "I mean, you had the whole Red Sox nation—including yours truly—clicking wildly that he should be fired for not taking out Pedro, and lo and behold, he gets fired for not taking out Pedro! Without my laptop, I'd have felt disenfranchised.

"Let me put it this way," added Altman. "Would you rather answer a poll about who should be the starting center for the Hornets, than actually watch the Hornets, yes or no?" ■

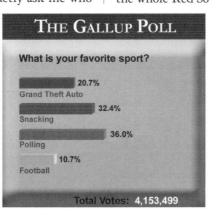

THE GALLUP POLL

What is your favorite sport?

20.7%
Grand Theft Auto

32.4%
Snacking

36.0%
Polling

10.7%
Football

Total Votes: 4,153,499

We scour the web so you don't have to.

Our pick for the best sports item available this month.

LOOKY HERE! You are bidding on a set of WILSON PRO STAFF GOLF CLUBS!!! TOP OF THE LINE! Some famous PGA tour pros use Wilsons! Great clubs here, minor wear and tear, go ahead and BID! You won't regret it! Details below.

Set includes carbon/titanium hybrid oversized 400cc performance driver, plus 3 and 5 Nano Tech fairway woods, four steel-shaft irons, and mallet-style putter. Driver slightly bent, some minor scuffs and nicks and blood. 7-iron features reduced offset and narrow sole for maximum versatility, and has flecks of brain embedded in club face. Weight-adjustable putter is designed to reduce jerks and yips, when free of scalp residue and gray matter.

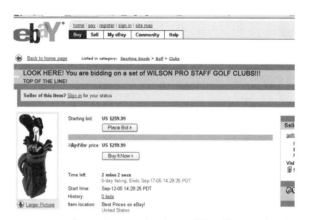

Irons have been rigorously cleaned (no fingerprints!) but might need regripping. Set was used just twice, once on golf course.

Where we spotlight those who talk about those who do

Legendary sports talk host Joe Broglio recently retired after 46 years. Here's a call from his final night on the air.

Late-Night Sports Radio Call

New York, September 30, 3:09 A.M. Host: Joe Broglio

Uh, yeah. Hi, Joe. I'm a first-time/long-time, thanks for taking the call, I was on hold for, like, three, four, hours there. So there are . . . um, three things I wanted to talk about . . . [*fumbling, rustling of papers*] Uh, POINT NUMBER ONE, okay? Point number one, the Rangers. My GOD, Joe, the Rangers. They're HORRIBLE! They're 1-and-4 in the preseason, they look just terrible . . . so I think they're, you know . . . done for the year, basically. But I LOVE hockey, so I wanted to hear your top three teams in the NHL for this year. I got [*fum-*

> ### [*fumbling, rustling of papers*] Uh, POINT NUMBER ONE, okay? Point number one.

bling] St. Louis 1, Minnesota 2, the Flyers 3. And I, uh, wanted to hear what you . . . uh, y'know . . . y'know, thought there. Ummmm . . . [*fumbling*] okay, POINT NUMBER TWO is the Mets. Willie Randolph is KILLIN' us, Joe. I STILL can't believe Lou Piniella didn't come here. Can't believe it! LOU PINIELLA BELONGS IN NEW YORK, JOE. TRUST ME! And instead, he was a nobody in TAMPA BAY! You ever been to Tampa, Joe? What a dump. I wouldn't even put Tampa in my top 20 cities. AND he was stuck managin' the absolute WORST team on the PLANET, Joe, the Devil Rays! Can you believe it? Or as I like to call 'em, the Devil GAYS, HAHA ha . . . ehh. It's like my cousin Larry, Joe. He leaves home—a GOOD home, Joe, a good home—and he gets in with the Buddhists. Can you believe it? The BUDDHISTS, Joe! Me, I got Christian 1, Jewish 2 . . . Buddhist I don't even got top five. I'd love to hear your top three there, with the uh . . . y'know, the religions there . . . Okay . . . [*rustling of papers*] That's all I got. Thanks for your time, Joe, love the show. Bye. ∎

Basketball Star Buys Own Team

Practice canceled

Billy Steele, star forward for the New Jersey Nets, has become the NBA's first player/owner.

"The deal just made a lot of sense," explained Steele's agent, Jeremy Golus. "By leveraging his salary and sneaker endorsements, Billy was able to buy his own contract, as well as the contracts of his teammates and the coaching staff, and still have enough left over to foot the stadium lease and NBA franchise fee."

In the team's press conference announcing the sale, Steele said that the purchase of his former employer was a dream come true.

"I never liked having a boss, you know?" said Steele, beaming. "I think when you work for yourself, you work harder. I'm excited."

Steele becomes the first player/majority owner in team sports history. "I'm my generation's Curt Flood," said Steele. "Only this playa writes the checks."

Steele declared that the team could expect wholesale changes, including the termination of head coach Alvin Ross, effective immediately. Ross, a noted disciplinarian, had openly feuded with Steele about the player's punctuality and work ethic.

"Coach is fired, no severance," said Steele. "His staff too. Y'all saw that Cavs game where they left me on the bench for the final five minutes. This is a business."

Steele said that the franchise would be expected to turn a profit as early as this year, and that due to cost-cutting and team chemistry concerns, he would most likely not be hiring a new coach.

"I just dropped $650 million of my own coin," said

"Besides, whatever issues we got we can work out during the game."

Steele. "Ask me about paying for things like a coach and a trainer some other day.

"Personally, I feel there's no need for babysitters— players can take care of themselves," Steele said. "That's why I'm canceling all practices from here on out. They're murder on the utility bills. Besides, whatever issues we got we can work out on the court during the first half. NBA games always come down to the last five minutes anyway." Steele then headed to the locker room, where he informed teammates that, as their teammate/owner/coach and union representative, he would be working from home.

Some of Steele's teammates appeared upset.

"Look, it's his decision," said forward Antonio Medwar, after Steele had departed. "But he's gonna go kick it in the owner's suite whenever he gets in foul trouble?" ■

TRIVIA CORNER

ORIGINAL FRANCHISE NAMES

MIAMI HEAT: Miami Humidity
NEW JERSEY NETS: New Jersey Asbestos
WASHINGTON REDSKINS: Washington Savage Featherheads
NEW YORK METS: Hymietown Mets

Our correspondents keep their ears open and their recording devices on

We took note as Yuba City, Calif., Community College football coach Otis Fretwell addressed his charges at halftime of a recent game.

Playa's Coach

Y ou call yourselves a football team? We're up by three at the half, and I don't see one guy prancing around curling his biceps. Not one guy! It's like you're a buncha drones. Where's the personality? Where's the flava?

Perkins, what kinda shit is that, just handin' the ball to the ref? It was third and two and you got four yards. PLAY LIKE A PLAYA, PLAYA! Pound your chest. Break that dance routine out for the whole world to see. There's 35 seconds between plays—plenty of time for The Worm.

On D, we're makin' plays—two turnovers—but we ain't stampin' our mark on 'em! God forbid you guys nail the quarterback and CELEBRATE for once. We've racked up three sacks this afternoon and not one memorable sack dance.

On O, your high fives are sloppy, your fist bumps lack vigor. Punctuate your preening with an exaggerated first-down signal. Make it crisp—Palmer, that was the lamest hand-chop I've seen all year. You had a 12-yard gain! Where's the showmanship? Where's your sense of the moment?

Pop your jersey when you get a first down. Even if it's by penalty, let the fans at home know it was you who was in on or near the play.

To paraphrase the legendary Paul Brown: If you take it to the hizzy, act like you've never bizzeen there before! Fo' shizzle!

And I don't care what the damn score is—if you make a good play, HEY, YOU MADE A GOOD PLAY! Pour some honey on it. Let the people know. Push teammates away so the cameras can get a clear shot as you pound your chest.

Remember what we talked about after last week's loss: Focus on the details. Is your shirt tucked in or out? Out is more intimidating, in looks better during night games.

I don't like to see penalties, but if you have to take off your helmet to argue with a ref, by all means take off your helmet. Show you care. We gotta make an impression here.

Don't forget, you can't spell team without M and E.

And here's a thought: How about coming up with something new? Moon-walking went out two decades ago. Yeah, I know, that would require homework, film study, watching MTV—all the things the coaching staff has been preaching. It's too late for that now, men, but like I been saying all week: Everybody remembers the game when T.O. pulled a Sharpie out of his sock; nobody remembers who won.

Now, everyone grab something to whip out if we score again. A towel, a glow-stick, a trophy from high school, whatever. Tuck it in your shorts.

All right men, five minutes until the second half. Let's work on my Gatorade bath. ∎

Victoria Whipperscrap, 63, is a lecturer for the Royal Horticultural Society and the author of The Concise Encyclopedia and Photo-Library of Ornamental Plants, *vols. I–XXIV. She recently shared her thoughts with* SMTM *on her first 10 months on the job.*

Madison Square Gardener

BY VICTORIA WHIPPERSCRAP

On the whole I'd have to say the job has been a dollop of a disappointment. Perhaps more than a dollop. I came here from the grounds of Chatsworth House in Derbyshire, where I was master horticulturalist for 17 years. My orchids were renowned from Cornwall to Leicester.

Alas, the fabled gardens of Madison Square are primarily of the beer variety!

They lured me here with much ballyhoo, I daresay. "Madison Square Garden is the world's most famous arena!" and such. Well, I'm one for adventure, and who wouldn't want to tend the most visited garden in all New York? So I thought I'd give it a whirl, hop the pond.

Alas, the fabled gardens of Madison Square are primarily of the beer variety!

Twice a week I water the ferns in the Knicks' offices. Wednesdays it's to the Rangers' press room to dust the plastic ficus.

When the circus comes to town, I harvest fertilizer.

Indeed.

But it's not all rubbish, not on your Nelly.

Aside from the rather unpleasant weekend of the Westminster show, I don't have to deal with dogs on leads mucking up the camellia groves—as happened when I was curator of Abbotsbury.

After three weeks of deep depression, plus a losing streak for the Knickerbockers that stretched eight contests, I was ready to take the next lorry home to Bournemouth. But then, the seasons turned. As is their wont.

Hence, things are looking up. I've begun rhododendrons in the ladies' loo. Barely room to swing a tabby in there, particularly during Liberty games, but buds are beginning to break soil. And I've planted window boxes of annuals in the corporate suites. Just darling!

When I take a job, I'm in for a penny, in for a pound. ∎

Our recurring feature in which we revisit the sports lore of simpler times, via the *SMTM* archives

Rush Limbaugh: White Quarterbacks Suffering In Obscurity

Conservative talk show host Rush Limbaugh, who resigned from his job as football commentator for ESPN in June, last month expanded on his charge that Eagles All-Pro quarterback Donovan McNabb receives undue media support because of his skin color.

"Everywhere I look it's Tony Banks this, Andre Ware that," said Limbaugh during his daily radio show. "The media has been so desirous that a black quarterback do well, you can hardly open a newspaper without seeing some sportswriter fawning over [1988 West Virginia QB] Major Harris.

"Meanwhile, white guys like Drew Bledsoe and Peyton Manning—you may have seen them play on cable—can't even get a TV interview because the politically correct media are all lining up to speak with [1988 Super Bowl MVP] Doug Williams."

Continued Limbaugh: "You don't hear anything about Jeremy Shockey, one of the game's best unheralded young white players. Why? Because Shockey has the misfortune to play football in the United States, where all the media attention goes to [Arizona Cardinals' second-stringer] Jeff Blake. It's institutionalized reverse-racism.

"Everywhere I look it's Tony Banks this, Andre Ware that."

"Take Akili Smith," continued Limbaugh. "He got cut from the Bengals and the Packers this year, and now he's out of football. But just because he's a black quarterback, Katie Couric and Barbara Walters practically live in his family room. Meanwhile, Brett Favre has to pour his Wheaties out of a box with [former NFL/USFL journeyman] Vince Evans on it. It's wrong."

"Yesterday, the Chiefs beat the Broncos in a huge matchup, and the Cubs won their first postseason series in almost a century," said Limbaugh, holding up the current issue of *Sports Illustrated.* "But who's on the cover here? You guessed it: [retired Saskatchewan Rough Riders QB] Reggie Slack." ■

THIS MONTH IN HISTORY
October 19, 1964
Advent of instant replay renders paid sideline re-enactors obsolete.

October 3, 1965
Yanks' manager lets fading Mickey Mantle bat, drink fifth.

VOLUME 100, NO. 12

NOVEMBER

SPORTS MAGAZINE

THE MAGAZINE

TEXAS HOCKEY TEAM INSTITUTES DEATH PENALTY BOX

ISBN 1-4000-9795-9

9 781400 097951

Lone Star Squad Administering "Ultimate Penalty"

In an effort to curtail escalating on-ice misconduct, the NHL's Dallas Stars this week instituted the league's first death penalty box.

"We got tired of seeing our best players roughed up by no-talent thugs," explained Stars GM Doug Armstrong, "only to have some candy-ass liberal ref set these guys free five minutes later."

Now, at all Stars home games, anyone charged with a major penalty, such as spearing or cross-checking, is assessed a "strike." Once a player accumulates three strikes, he is immediately escorted to a sterile 6'-by-6' ringside box outfitted with a high-back chair and leather straps. Justice is served.

The idea seems to be a crowd-pleaser.

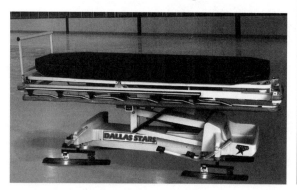

Penalty minutes have declined 31 percent since the introduction of the death penalty box, and many fans at American Airlines Center note that action on the ice has become more fluid, with far fewer bare-knuckle brawls.

"It's more of a European game in here now," said Stars season ticket holder Robert Gibson, wearing blue jeans and an Ulf Dahlen jersey. "By the third period, most of the remaining players are quick little blue-eyed wingers with good stick skills. Except for the national anthem and the acrid stench of burning flesh, you'd think you were in Finland, not central Texas."

Many of the league's worst offenders have already been terminated, to the delight of the crowd.

"Tie Domi gave us his final power play, all right," chuckled Gibson, referring to the Maple Leafs' notorious goon, "About 2,000 volts' worth."

"Everyone's always whining about the violence in hockey," said Stars chairman Tom Hicks, who dreamed up the idea, "but we're actually doing something about it."

A rare exception in league policy, the three-strikes rule, explained Hicks, is necessary to combat hockey's high rate of recidivism.

"Everyone's always whining about the violence in hockey, but we're actually doing something about it."

"A lot of these guys were chronic offenders. They'd serve their time for one offense, like high-sticking, and wind up right back in the box for another. You can either try to rehabilitate people like that—the costs of which would force us to raise ticket prices—or you can eliminate them."

Research into Texas's arcane criminal punishment laws confirmed that the Stars' private enforcement of a death penalty is, in fact, completely legal. However, not all have embraced the idea.

Outside the arena, protester Nancy Gratz distributed candles and poems dedicated to recently executed players.

"This just isn't fair," she said. "And how come a disproportionate number of those put to death have been Blackhawks?" ■

TV Picks

[**8:00**] ESPN Classic—4/7/01 Episode of *Battlebots*
[**9:30**] PAX—*God's Favorite Touchdowns*
[**11:00**] ESPN2—*Extreme TV-Watching* (live from Norway)

New Fitness Craze: Impersonal Trainers

NEWS IN BRIEF

Halftime Pep Talk Marred By Historical Inaccuracies

Amateur Olympics Formed

Joyous Dodge Owners Riot Across Nation After Kasey Kahne Win

Salvation Army/Navy Game Ends In Paisley Tie

CORRECTIONS

Our tribute to the life of Pat Tillman should not have included nine paragraphs on Mark Cuban and a free Terrell Owens trading card.

For 18th Straight Year, Gamblers Try Unsuccessfully To Fix World Series

It's not easy being a big-time gambler these days. As the industry has become increasingly mainstreamed—with more and more states legalizing various forms of betting, and the proliferation of online gambling—those who grew up in the business aren't thriving like they used to. And attempts to fix the World Series have failed, according to underworld gamblers, for nearly 20 consecutive years.

"I think the general public makes the mistake of assuming that the infamous fix of the 1919 'Black Sox' Series was an anomaly, a dark day in an otherwise rosy century," says baseball historian John Thorn. "But I can assure you, the players have not gotten less corrupt; they have simply gotten much, much richer."

Explains Johnny "Squeaky" Lippmann, great-grandson of Robert Lippmann, one of the key figures in the 1919 fix: "In my great-grandpa's day, ballplayers earned peanuts for a living. Hard as it is to imagine, back then most big leaguers actually had to work winter jobs to put food on the table. So when gamblers would approach a guy with an offer of three grand, that was an enormous deal. They were jumping out of their chairs to say yes. I mean, really, a six-year-old could have fixed the Series back then—if he had the dough.

> **"Today they make about 40 times the average salary. So what the hell are you gonna offer these guys? Love? I tried that once. No takers."**

"But like the game itself, the fixing of games has changed. Baseball purists point to the designated hitter as the death knell of the game as they knew it; gamblers point to free agency. In the early part of the century ballplayers earned three, four times the average working man's salary. Today they make about 40 times the average salary. So what the hell are you gonna offer these guys? Love? I tried that once. No takers."

Salvatore Fornario, another underworld figure, tells of his ill-fated attempt to fix a recent World Series: "I get to talking with this pitcher—he's the third starter in the rotation, I figure he's a good guy to work because the scrutiny would be on the other guys, the superstars. I ask him, 'You wanna make an easy three mil?' The guy loses it. I mean, just flat-out cracks up—he's rolling on the floor. When he regains his breath, he tells me that was his signing bonus as a rookie. I felt like such a damn mook."

Because no amount of money seems to suffice, gamblers have tried making less conventional offers. Said Fornario, "One time I nearly pulled it off. I put together this real nice package for a guy who had off-field troubles—complete guaranteed cover-ups of all his misdemeanors and affairs, foolproof alibis, the works. But in the end I decided it wasn't worth it for me—you know how much it costs to make all that stuff happen? I would have had to hire five people to cover all his tracks."

Says Lippmann, "We might not be villains in the court of public opinion, but believe me, in my family I'm a total failure. My aunt Louise is always saying, 'Your great-grandpa could fix anything—World Series, title fight, you name it. But you? You couldn't fix a mid-June Devil Rays game.'" ■

AIRWAVES

Where we spotlight those who talk about those who do

Contestant Theo Neukomm, 12, was favored by many experts to win the annual Scripps National Spelling Bee last month. Following is Theo's exit from the bee in the final round.

National Spelling Bee, Transcript

Moderator: The word is "encephalic."

Neukomm: Definition, please.

Related to the brain.

The brain, eh? Gotta love the brain. Okay, let's see. E . . . uh . . . hmm . . . nation of origin, please?

Greece.

Nice! My uncle loves Greek food. Brings it over all the time.

Please spell your word.

I am, I am! E . . . uh . . . N . . . uh . . . any alternate pronunciations?

No.

Never hurts to check. Where was I? Oh yeah: E . . . —whoa—any umlauts or anything goofy like that I should be aware of?

One minute remaining.

Geez. Okay . . . let's see here . . . E-N . . . uh . . . Excuse me, can you say the word again, please?

Encephalic.

Cool. Any antonyms?

No.

Homonyms?

No.

Can you spell it for me?

Can I spell it for you? Of course not.

Right! Didn't think you'd go for that, but what the hey. Worth a try. What's the second vowel? E?

You have 30 seconds.

Any silent letters? I hate those. Gnocchi. What's the point of the g?

Ten seconds. Please finish spelling the word.

Okay, okay. E-N-C-uh . . . hang on a sec. Lost my train of thought.

Five seconds.

Take it easy, pal! I'm on TV here. ■

Title IX Augmented By Measure 36-24-36

Revised rule lets schools offer both women's and ladies' sports

Title IX, the federal law passed over 30 years ago to give equal opportunities to female athletes, underwent a historic transformation today as a congressional advisory commission passed Measure 36-24-36. The action allows schools to enhance their often unprofitable female athletic programs with sports like Jell-O Wrestling and Foxy Boxing.

Commission member Frank Jonas explained the significance of the decision: "Until now, most schools have been able to meet Title IX by simply paring men's programs and adding sparsely attended women's sports like archery.

"But now, rather than being forced to cut nonrevenue male sports like wrestling, schools can add high-revenue female sports. Like wrestling."

The new ruling was met with mostly positive reactions.

Jenna Karp, a junior at Georgetown University, expressed relief and optimism: "This is a big day for many, many students. Until now I'd been forced to pursue my oil wrestling career on my own time, at off-campus venues like Kitty-Kat and The Spank Bank. With Measure 36-24-36, my participation

UCLA vs. USC

will finally be supported by the administration, the NCAA . . . maybe even my family."

Stan Minnaugh, athletic director at Randolph High School in Arlington, Va., was also enthusiastic. "This just opens so many doors for so many young scholar-stripper-athletes," he said. "Now, if I've got a sophomore who's interested in pursuing scholarships for both lacrosse and caged heat [in which contestants don catsuits and claw at each other in a suspended cage], she's got options."

Feminist organizations appeared surprisingly ambivalent. Said Diane Glass, a spokesperson for the National Organization for Women, "It's hard to get worked up over this. I mean, even if we *somehow* were to get this measure overturned, women would still be portrayed as sex objects in 9 out of 10 Hollywood movies, cereal commercials, tennis matches . . . Believe me, we've got a long to-do list. You've gotta choose your battles.

"And let's not forget, economic gains have always been one of feminism's chief objectives. Now, with this single decision, the revenue from men's and women's basketball *combined* will be virtually equaled by that of pajama-party pillow-fighting." ■

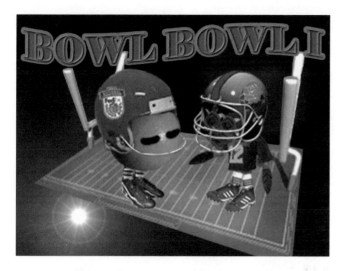

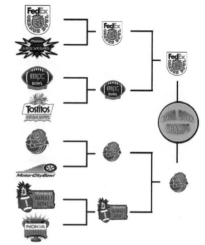

Bowl System Solved By Bowl Bowl

The NCAA is proud to announce its solution to college football's controversial system of determining a champion. In the style of the popular Bud Bowl series, the Bowl Bowl is an animated simulation tournament between the 28 sanctioned bowl games. The winner of the Bowl Bowl will decide the national championship.

Says NCAA Bowl Bowl producer Marty Sabath, "The two most common complaints we hear are that the national champion is determined by computer, and that TV viewers don't know which of dozens of bowl games to actually watch. Now, thanks to innovative graphics and punchy art direction, both problems are solved. The Bowl Bowl is one-stop shopping for the college football fan."

The use of animation—with teams represented by cuddly or cartoonishly menacing "football playing characters" including Gators, sacks of Sugar, and tiny MPC Computers—adds a fun, family-friendly ingredient. The vibrant Rose Bowl/Emerald Bowl matchup, for one, promises to be visually stunning.

What's more, the Bowl Bowl features maximum realism, as every first-round contest is between a powerhouse like the Sugar Bowl and an unseeded underdog like the Fort Worth Bowl. But thanks to the NCAA's crack Bowl Bowl writing staff, compelling upsets are guaranteed. Be sure to watch the second-round game between the third-seeded Cotton Bowl and the lightly regarded squad of the Continental Tire Bowl, the Fighting Tire-ish.

Bowl Bowl I airs January 8 on ABC, beginning with *Road to the Bowl Bowl* at 3:30 P.M. EST.

We scour the Web so you don't have to

The following message board, found on profootballchat.com, is our pick for best recent online NFL discussion.

Football Message Board

Wednesday, November 5, 4:40 P.M. EST

FirstAndFifteen: Hey when r the latest power rankings posted on ESPN.com? If Saints pull #25 again I'm a bust a nut! F*ck those writers with their rankings! Anybody know what time they come out? I been checking but nothing yet.

JimCrashJensen: I don't know what time but I know '72 Dolpins greatest #1 team all time case closed.

Shockey43: lmfao! fins suk.

MikeinMahopac: Looking for good place to buy bulk aluminum siding. Please advise.

DrBiletnikoff: CALLING OUT SHOCKEY 43 FOR BEING A DIK-HEAD.

Shockey43: Bring it on, bitch.

[]D[][]v[][]D: Dolphins were a sham—no competition that year. Put any of the last ten SB winners up against them. Only close game would be Broncos '98.

Phillyfan77: Bullsh*t! Gang green in da house!

Administrator: Please remember the rules of engagement for this forum. Cursing is not allowed.

dawglb: Do not use aluminum siding use vinyl siding better insulator, cheaper in long run.

Shockey43: Sorry. Just trying to make DrBiletnikoff put his $ where his piehole is at.

DrBiletnikoff: Anytime, anywhere.

emart88: Have you tried Home Depot?

Shockey43: OK. Where are you? I'll kick you're bitchy little ass. I'm in Phoenix. 3 N. Central Ave. 12th floor. Suite #1233. Corner office, punk.

Grange58: One item to consider, when comparing the proficiency of teams in the modern era, is yards per pass play. YPP is a key indicator in determining offensive efficiency. To wit, the 1972 Dolphins were quite productive in this regard: Earl Morrall and Bob Griese quarterbacked them to an 8.63 average. Bear in mind that this is long before the league tracked yardage lost via sacks. Just my two cents.

threeandacloud: Everybody better stop drinking the Haterade around here!

dawglb: Ho Depot sux! Filthy, workers unhappy, like being at a Raiders game. Commitment To Sucking.

stiffarm22: Anybody watch Chicago Hope last nite?

MikeinMahopac: I did go to HD emart88, thanks. Couldn't find right color finish. looking to re-side an old barn, prefer to use aluminum.

DrBiletnikoff: Admin.: I sent you an e-mail about Shockey43 two weeks ago. He just comes on here to flame everyone.

BubbyToWeegieFor6: Yo! Steeltown! why didn't Cowher call a timout against Jints in '92 MNF game? just asking ok thanks I LOVE THIS SITE!!!!!!

Patronym: Hi all! I'm back! Thanks for the kind wishes. Very tough, close call. Surgery went well. Really missed everybody! Hoping to get feeling back

in limbs. Blessed to be alive. Eagles fans are fags!

Phillyfan77: Cowher had used his timeouts already, in third quarter. I have game tape.

RonMexico65: People posting on this forum are lozers with no lifes!

TrentMilfer: Hi folks kick ass mess board! Funny story: You know how fans sometimes have little superstitious stuff they do to help their team win? Like my mom always wears her lucky Indians hat? I figured out that every time I pleasure myself at some during the first half of a Pats game, we win. If I don't we lose. Man, it's been one hell of a ride! Believe you me, this has not been easy. The worst was '98 v. Buffalo. There I was, in the men's room at Foxboro, freezing my a** off, hundreds of guys waiting in line behind me, Pats down by a touchdown and well, let's just say it took a while for the offense to get going! My hands were all chapped. Anyway, long story short, we won by 4.

Groinpull55: Y'all crazee—Bears '85 were da shiznizzle. Woulda pushed '72 Fins around like girlies. Check out this link awesome dumb blond jokes www.partylaffs.com PEACE!

threeandacloud: Hi everybody boss says no message boards on worktime WTF is up with that? Cowher's gay—call a timeout already. Go to Lowe's—better pricing better service I'm out CHIEFS RULE ALL EYEZ ON DA RED AND WHITE THIS WEEKEND!

FirstAndFifteen: Hey anybody seen the latest NFL power rankings on ESPN.com?? When they come out?

TV Cameras Now Everywhere

Latest wireless fiber-optics offer total sports immersion

◀ Ball cam
Splitter or slider? Now we know for sure.

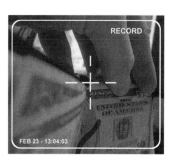

Owner's wallet cam ▶
Bottom of the eighth, five-game lead in the standings evaporating, watch first hand as George Steinbrenner's black leather tri-fold blooms open, exposing the green fields within, and a call is placed to the Kansas City Royals' GM.

◀ Throat cam
About the size of a lozenge, the throat cam lets viewers see the game from where it originates: inside the coach's mouth. Hear pitching changes ruminating through a ball of chaw. See spittle well up in anger long before being discharged on the umpire's foot. If swallowed, the eucalyptus-flavored device passes harmlessly through the user's body in a few days, and doubles as a cordless endoscope.

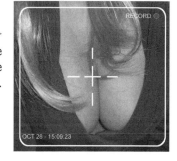

Bra cam ▶
Rather than the traditional horizontal pan of cheerleaders shot from the waist up, the bra cam brings game day cleavage to HD. Boom-mounted on a scoop-neck blouse and aimed nippleward, the zoom-enabled device is no bigger than a lapel pin.

◀ Cam cam
Ever wonder who or what's behind the camera? Now you can thrill to the facial stubble and polyester T-shirts of our best action photogs.

Where we invite our readers to go head-to-head on today's hot-button sports issues

Olympic Medals Should Be Retroactively Awarded To Minorities Denied A Chance To Compete

BY RUTH BADER GINSBURG

I know it's unusual for a Supreme Court justice to write in to a sports publication, and in such an uncharacteristically chatty tone, no less. Precedent exists, however (see William Rehnquist's letter demanding the cancellation of his *Sports Illustrated* subscription, in response to an "insufficiently racy" swimsuit issue, 2/13/81).

Anyhoo, usually I do my public opining via arcane legal opinions. But when an issue is this dear to my heart, and there are no federal cases pertaining to it on the horizon, I cannot stay quiet.

For too long, America denied the inherent right to compete to the full spectrum of its citizens. Be it via institutional racism or gender bias, for much of our nation's

athletic history, equality of opportunity was but a chimera.

So what shall we say to those potential swim racing champions—some of whom were never even taught to swim—who happened to be, say, African American in 1952? "Sorry, the gold medal in

the 100-meter freestyle at Helsinki is still unattainable?"

In a democratic republic, that's not good enough. As Frederick Douglass (who possessed a breathtakingly fluid backstroke, I'm told) once wrote, "The life of a nation is secure only while the nation is honest, truthful, and virtuous."

That's why we must right these past five-ring wrongs.

How, you ask?

Reparations. Specifically, the awarding of Olympic medals to all those likely to have won them, had they been given the opportunity to swim competitively in their youth, as say, Mark Spitz was.

The cost?

Minimal (I'm told Olympic medals aren't actually made of precious metals, but cheap tinted alloy). Furthermore, if we begin with the advent of the modern Olympic Games in 1896, we need only identify a single century's worth of potential champs. (Not just champs—let's be fair to the silvers and bronzes too.)

By what methodology will we discern past winners?

Genetic probability. The technology now exists, through DNA analysis of bones and hair strands, to glean a general sense of one's inherent athletic ability, even if the subject has crumbled nearly to dust. Once samples are obtained, the questions to ask are obvious: When living, how high could this person have jumped in 1904? Would that have qualified for an Olympic medal? Could such and such corpse have possessed the eyesight and muscle tone, while alive, that would have provided an advantage in shooting events? What about decathlon? And for those as-yet-unidentified athletes who are still with us, questions such as: This person is now old and frail, but could he or she have captured any discus medals in Melbourne in 1956?

So here's to Judith Lee Abbey, probable 100-meter hurdles winner, Antwerp, 1920. And Rafer Williams, who might have captured bronze in Oslo in 1952, had he been allowed his constitutional right to a pair of skis and a giant-slalom coach.

America's unsung, unwitting, and sometimes long-dead sports stars must be unearthed and given their due. Justice delayed is justice denied. ■

Ruth Bader Ginsburg is a U.S. Supreme Court justice.

No

By Clarence Thomas

I disagree. ■

Clarence Thomas is a U.S. Supreme Court justice.

Photo: Joyce Naltchayan/AFP/Getty Images

Our correspondents are always on the lookout for noteworthy sports artifacts

This month, an excerpt from an advance copy of Ken Burns's highly anticipated documentary of the XFL.

When We Were Maniax

A FILM BY KEN BURNS, NARRATED BY DAVID MCCULLOUGH

Production made possible by grants from the World Wrestling Federation's Endowment for the Humanities

Part 1 of 13

Opening shot: *Sunrise over fields, silhouette of Civil War cannons, sounds of distant gunfire, coaches' whistle.*
Narrator [*hushed, awed tone*]: "We have shared the incommunicable experience of war. We have felt, we still feel, the passion of life to its top. In our youth, our hearts were touched by fire." Oliver Wendell Holmes.

Dissolve to photo of He Hate Me.

Narrator: In the year 2000, reformists gained control of the Iranian parliament, and a spacecraft orbited an asteroid for the first time. Here in America, Kathie Lee Gifford retired. From its inception in February, until its demise barely more than a year later, the upstart XFL struggled to capture the nation's heart. Backed by little more than grit, shoe polish, three television networks, and 100 million dollars, the ragtag football league began with the promise of spring.

Interview: Dr. Priscilla Lehman-Livingston, M.I.T., author of *Only the Ball Was Black and Red.* "Back then this country needed a diversion from the fighting in Sierra Leone. It was on everybody's mind, every TV channel. The NFL and college football seasons run from August until early February, and Arena Football runs from late March through July. So there was a six-week period in which the American people might have had to watch coverage of a foreign tribal conflict, or go outside. The XFL stepped in to fill that void. It was a very patriotic, noble mission."

Dissolve to photo of Vince McMahon.

XFL clubs stood for things real: violence, mob rule, poor spelling. The new league boasted Hitmen, Outlaws, and Maniax.

Narrator: Ringleader Vince McMahon was America's fin-de-siècle answer to P. T. Barnum: a showman with a common touch.

Said McMahon, "If I have a gift, it's that I know what the average Joe Sixpack wants."

Dissolve to T&A cheerleader shot no. 1.

Narrator: In a move Barnum would have much admired, the letter *X* in XFL had no meaning. It was chosen because it looked marketable. More fan-friendly tactics followed.

Dissolve to T&A cheerleader shot no. 2.

Narrator: McMahon eliminated many of the NFL's esoteric conventions, like coin flips and Roman numerals. Banished too were haughty team names like Patriots and Seahawks. XFL clubs stood for things real: violence, mob rule, poor spelling. The new league boasted Hitmen, Outlaws, and Maniax.

Team logo photos slow pan.

Narrator: The XFL's championship event was called the "Million Dollar Game" in a tip of the cap . . . to money!

"Million Dollar Game" shots.

Interview: Shelby Foote, late historian; author, *Xtreme Appomattox.* "A pair of imbroglios tarred the city of Memphis for quite a few years. When Dr. King was killed, of course, and when the Memphis Showboats, of the old USFL football circuit, folded up back in 1986. You see, some thought our way of life here was headed for the woodshed. Then the 'Ax came a-calling. It was a real step forward."

Fans in war paint photo fade-in.

Action photos of Maniax.

Narrator [*speaking over montage of fans, players, etc.*]: Sadly, like Woodrow Wilson's League of Nations, the XFL was an idealistic union the American people were not yet ready to accept. Just seven weeks into the season, an XFL game registered the lowest prime-time rating in TV history. The league soldiered on, but its spirit was broken. Cofounder NBC pulled its funding shortly after the Million Dollar Game. The XFL's moment had passed.

When asked to comment, most players declined, still too stunned that the Little Mega-League That Could, could not. Pounding his chest above the heart, former Birmingham Thunderbolt Calvin Jackson offered this: "I feel like Julius Caesar: tragic . . . and dead. Tragic and dead. Dead in my heart. Ever since the league died, I'm just dead to me."

Photo of Jackson with helmet on backwards and fade. ∎

Better Than The Original: "Super Bowl III: Director's Cut"

BY FRED MUCKPO

Classic sporting events improved by digital technology and brash, forceful editing? You better believe it! Just as TKO Sports' previous DVD release, *100 Years of Sportz!*, dramatically improved such hoary events as Kirk Gibson's World Series homer and the "Rumble in the Jungle," the new version of the New York Jets' legendary upset over the Baltimore Colts in 1969 is leaps and bounds better than the original.

"When we reviewed the masters of the original game," explains TKO Sports producer Gary Byrne in the superb commentary track included in *Super Bowl III—Director's Cut,* "we found they were lacking in vibrancy, the soundtrack hadn't aged well, and the players looked smaller and slower than they do today. In correcting the transfers for widescreen surround-sound presentation, we were also able to make some narrative enhancements—just a few little things that I think help make Super Bowl III a

cleaner, fresher, more fully realized story."

Thus, Matt Snell's ho-hum four-yard run—the Jets' only touchdown—has been digitally replaced by a scrambling, toe-dragging 45-yard back-of-the-end-zone bomb from Joe Namath to George Sauer.

Explains Byrne: "Although his stats were pretty modest, 206 passing yards and no TDs, Namath was named Super Bowl MVP. Thus, we felt that the original game, as played, really didn't tell an accurate story. In popular memory, Namath was no dink-and-dunk passer—he was a brash gunslinger who piled up big yardage. Thanks to imaging software, we are now able to give fans a version of Super Bowl III that meshes perfectly with its place in popular history."

Likewise, Sauer's early fumble in Jets territory, which was recovered by the Colts, has been completely removed in the new version. Says Byrne: "The fumble interrupted the narrative flow, and unfairly detracted from what was an efficient performance by the Jets' offense. It was, in a word, gratuitous."

Production quality is first-rate: The field is now a richer green, and you can more clearly see the lines on Weeb Ewbank's face.

To this reviewer, *Super Bowl III* blows Super Bowl III away. (The "classic" version, while a stunning upset, was also a 16–7 snoozer.) Broadway Joe made his famous guarantee from a poolside lounge chair at a Miami hotel days before the game, but it's far more compelling as presented here: on the field before kickoff, pointing into the camera, music swelling. This is clearly how it was meant to be. ■

Fred Muckpo, sports historian, is the author of Raging Bullsh*t: Sports in Cinema.

Marlins Return To Winter Jobs

After conquering the New York Yankees in the World Series, the scrappy Florida Marlins enjoyed a raucous, celebratory 19-hour ride home from the Bronx on the team's rented yellow school bus. Awaiting them in south Florida was a parade through downtown Miami, followed by a return to winter employment.

"Everyone thinks facing the Yankees is hard," said 23-year-old pitching phenom Josh Beckett, who shut down the high-priced Yankees lineup in the decisive sixth game. "But it's nothing compared to waking up at 4:30 to drive a milk truck every day from November 'til mid-February."

Jack McKeon, manager of the Marlins and of We All Scream, the Pensacola ice cream franchise, agreed. "It's tough to win the World Series without the payroll the Yankees have. But then, customer service is no picnic either. You can't appeal to the umpire when somebody's hassling you about how he didn't get enough sprinkles on his jumbo Scream-Dream."

A few lucky Marlins, however, can look forward to a winter relatively free of service work and manual labor. Jeff Conine, a 14-year Major League veteran, says those days are behind him. "Oh sure, for the first eight or nine years I was in the majors, I spent the off-seasons working 12-hour shifts at the car wash. But this year, I've got enough saved up that I only need to work part-time to make it to spring." ∎

THIS MONTH IN HISTORY

November 10, 1966
Bill Walton scores 19 points, 3 tabs in first-ever Electric Gatorade Acid Test.

November 13, 1982
Stanford marching band surrenders 217 kickoff yards, 2 TDs in loss at UCLA.

SPORTS MAGAZINE

THE MAGAZINE

SPECIAL
100TH ANNIVERSARY
RETROSPECTIVE

Riots, Hysteria Sweep Nation With Advent Of "Forward Pass"

New foot-ball play condemned by Supreme Court as obscene; President calls for Knute Rockne's arrest

DECEMBER, 1907

President Roosevelt has placed the country on "Highest Possible Level of Alert Regarding the Safety and Welfare of the Citizenry" as a result of the newly legalized foot-ball play in which the quarter-back tosses the ball past the line of scrimmage to a team-mate waiting to catch said ball.

The mere sight of a man lobbing a ball high and wobbly into the air toward a stationary, patiently waiting team-mate instantly elicits high-pitched squeals from the female spectatorship, most of whom have never seen anything so brazenly suggestive.

One quarter-back, Ernest Volin of the Canton Bulldogs, has learned to hurl the projectile in a fluid, "spiraling" motion; when he first unveiled this technique in an October game in Chicago, seven teen-age girls fainted on the spot and were instantly hospitalized. Another, apparently possessing more intestinal fortitude than her peers, demonstrated her approval by flinging her neck-scarf onto the playing-field, prompting the president's declaration of a national emergency.

It was only two years ago that President Roosevelt called for football's rulemakers to allow the forward pass, in an effort to make the game—which had seen 18 deaths and hundreds of serious injuries in 1905 alone as a result of dangerous plays like the "hurdle" and "flying wedge"—less perilous. But the president now concedes he completely failed to foresee the havoc that would be wrought: "I wanted a more open, less savage brand of foot-ball; but for every player's life that we save, it seems we lose five to ten civilians to shock and trauma, disproportionately women-folk.

"I am also told that the nation's young boys—so easily impressed by the actions of professional athletes and rag-time pianists—have descended into degeneracy: We are seeing record levels of truancy, cigarette smoking, and the reading of 'comic-books'—all the result of the anarchy unleashed by the forward pass."

The nation's two dozen sports-writers, always quick to affix a catchy "nick-name" to any new phenomenon, have dubbed the craze "The Widespread Fondness for the Forward Pass." ■

WOMEN'S EVENTS NO LONGER MEN IN DRAG

32 years after women's events debut at Olympics, Margaret Van Der Wahl becomes first woman to compete

AUGUST, 1932—To the dismay of many participants here at the Ninth Summer Olympiad in Los Angeles, the women's events at this year's Games have included several actual women.

"Confounded suffragists," cried longtime women's hurdler Howard Lincoln of Dover, Del., slumped on the side of the track in a turquoise chiffon blouse and navy skirt. "They already won the vote. Will they ever stop degrading the weaker sex?"

Although women have been competing in Olympic events such as golf and tennis since 1900, until now those women have been men.

"This is nothing less than an invitation to licentiousness and moral turpitude," said Britain's Richard Birdsall, applying fresh lipstick while awaiting his turn at the women's high jump. "Furthermore, scientists have proven that the limbs of our fair-skinned maidens will snap like twigs if subjected to the manly rigor of running at full speed."

Despite Birdsall's contention, Holland's Margaret Van Der Wahl emerged uninjured from the javelin competition, in which her toss of 43.68 meters won gold.

"White men have lost hundreds of jobs in the black minstrel industry to black performers over the past few years, and now this!" said women's tennis player and Providence, R.I., native George Matusow. "What's next? Students allowed to participate in high school sports, instead of their parents?"

Man Runs 5,280 Feet In Under 240 Seconds

Norman Potter/Hulton Archive/Getty Images

MAY, 1954—This month we were witness to an achievement that bounds from the sporting pages to the front pages with the same swiftness as its perpetrator.

It was England's Roger Bannister who made athletic and numeric history by becoming the first man ever to run 5,280 feet—a unit of measure preferred by one country in the world—in fewer than 240 seconds.

The most sacrosanct benchmark in all of sport, previously no mortal had run this distance—5,280 feet/1,609.347 meters/8 furlongs—in under 240 seconds. 241 seconds is unremarkable; 239 is legendary. Thus, by traveling at the rate of 1,760 yards in less than 1/15th of an hour, this heretofore-unknown Briton named Roger Bannister breached the magical point of delineation.

Now that this barrier has been broken, it seems the sky is the limit for all people and numbers. Whither the future? Perhaps a mortal will one day hurl a discus over 60,000 millimeters, or a javelin will soar 175 cubits!

This is a great and glorious day for units of measurement.

I Saw God And/Or Spurs V. Knicks

By Lester Bangs

FEBRUARY, 1979—Tonight's San Antonio/New York game was wild it was pure adrenaline it felt like Janis Joplin howling over late-era Coltrane, like a psychic fire burning for 48 minutes. It was so vivid and colorful I nearly cried. Big purple tears. New York's Ray Williams led all scorers with 27 points.

The first quarter was a slow, tentative waltz. Maddening, but arresting. Full of questions unanswered and glances snuck. Only 19 field-goal attempts in the entire period. Like two horny teenagers on the couch, not sure who's gonna make the first move and break that tension, that sublime awful tension that's only been building since we was embryos, since the dawn of time, since Eve took that fateful bite into the apple and . . . Spurs led 17–15 at the end of the period.

Second quarter gave me all kinds of flashbacks to being 6 years old, it was so pure and innocent and the sun was always shining and there was always milk and cookies on the kitchen table and every jump shot went in and you knew who your friends were and life made sense and both teams shot over 60 percent from the field.

Halftime. Shit man, halftime. It's like a four-letter word to me. Just hearing it makes my stomach knot up. 15-minute void. Not enough time to do anything, but too much time to do nothing. If I want to contemplate this cruel comedy we call life I can do it at 3 in the morning, in my bedroom, with a bottle of Irish whiskey and Lou Reed's *Metal Machine Music* on full blast. I don't need 15 minutes in the middle of a basketball game.

Tried to kill time in the men's room. Met this guy in there, said he recognized me. Said he had some peyote, and did I want to "watch the second half from the mezzanine section of Jupiter?" Told him I hadn't

> ## The third quarter was the mad crescendo, the multiple orgasm, the electric guitar ringing ungodly feedback and distortion through each fast break.

touched peyote in two years. Told him these days my only vices are black coffee and cigarettes. And liquor, and weed, and mushrooms and amphetamines and Robitussin. Finally agreed to just one button.

The third quarter was the mad crescendo, the multiple orgasm, the electric guitar ringing ungodly feedback and distortion through each fast break. Twelve turnovers in the quarter, seven lead changes. Pure animalistic chaos, the bliss of being alive, the fear of dying, the shadowy regions in between.

Fourth quarter. Comedown. Heavy, heavy comedown. Mind, body, soul barely recognize each other anymore, must reacquaint. Saw the sun setting over the Jumbotron with 3:04 remaining and New York ahead by seven. Remember thinking to myself: Might these "three minutes" last a lifetime? Might this in fact be some perverse Kafka-esque nightmare where three minutes really means half an hour? Due to lots of fouls and timeouts, it was.

Final score: New York 91, San Antonio 85. ∎

Lester Bangs (1949-1982), gonzo journalist and rock & roll poet, is considered the godfather of modern rock criticism.

Gnip Gnop Champ Wins Miniature Yhport

MOST MEMORABLE UNIFORMS

- 1946 Cleveland Indians cap with feather headdress
- 1972 Minnesota Vikings helmet with mounted walrus tusks
- 1975 Houston Astros multicolor jersey, rainbow wig
- 1976 Chicago White Sox shorts/ cummerbund/bow-tie ensemble
- 1983 Atlanta Hawks Speedo shorts
- 1988 Junior Dixon, sponsorless NASCAR driver
- 1993 Dallas Cowboy Cheerleaders silver star nipple tassels

Ken Levine/Getty Images Sport/Getty Images

Rise Of Young Black Stars Shows Success Can Be Achieved By All Prodigies

September, 1999—We are witnessing a revolution in sports. With the astonishing ascent of Tiger Woods in golf and Venus and Serena Williams in tennis, these previously lily-white sports are finally learning what other sectors of society have known for years: Skin color is irrelevant when you're vastly more talented than everyone else.

The success of these amazing young athletes gives hope to people of all colors and backgrounds. The message they send is an exhilarating one: No matter where you come from or what you look like, you too can achieve anything if you have one-in-a-billion talent and an obsessive father who's been programming you for his favorite sport since before you were born.

These young stars are a breath of fresh air, and a reminder of what sports are all about: That everyone has an equal opportunity to excel—except the freakishly talented, who have a much greater than equal opportunity.

VOLUME 100, NO. 14

DECEMBER

SPORTS MAGAZINE

THE MAGAZINE

MILLIONAIRES HONORED FOR PLAYTIME SKILLS

ISBN 1-4000-9795-9

Work, School Suspended To Commemorate Best At Leisure Pursuit

In a ceremony filled with the pomp traditionally reserved for returning war veterans, 25 semi-local multimillionaires were treated to an overwhelming display of praise, as the city gave raucous thanks for their proficiency at a child's game.

"This is a great day in the history of our city," gushed the mayor to a crowd of cheering citizens, most of them low-wage workers who, unwittingly, will pay for the big event via an upcoming tax increase, combined with a slight reduction in municipal bus service.

For proving themselves more adept at skills like tossing a ball and whacking it with a stick than any other group of millionaires assembled within the past 12 months, each member of the honored team was showered with confetti and given a ceremonial key to the city. Although none of the recipients actually lives in the city honoring them—preferring to reside in vast estates thousands of miles away—for practical reasons most stay in nearby hotels, condos, and gated rental communities on a seasonal basis.

From their heavily guarded parade procession, many of those honored took time to thank the working- and lower-class members cheering wildly for them; some offered eye contact and even the occasional wave. For such gestures they were roundly saluted. Their work, enjoyed by kindergartners during recess period the world over, will not begin again for another five months. ▪

Many of those honored took time to thank the working- and lower-class members cheering wildly for them; some offered eye contact and even the occasional wave.

Great-Grandson Of Seabiscuit Loses Again

"Cornbread" cementing reputation as lazy, shiftless heir

FUK: New Space Invaders High Score (2nd AAA, 3rd FUK)

Al Davis Mistakenly Sues, Countersues Self

Latest grievance names "Al Davis" for failure to provide team with adequate practice and malpractice facilities

Perhaps unhinged by the burden of managing multiple lawsuits, Oakland Raiders owner Al Davis unwittingly subpoenaed himself last month. Upon receiving the grievance—in which the owner charged himself with breach of contract—a furious Davis announced he would countersue.

"These allegations are baseless," said Davis, holding up a copy of *Davis v. Davis.* "I have done everything in my power to provide this team with top-notch players, coaches, and legal personnel."

The remarks occurred during a hastily assembled press conference at Raiders headquarters. Wearing a dark track suit and flashing several Super Bowl rings, the notoriously litigious owner—whose football team fled Los Angeles amid a flurry of lawsuits and has since sued every one of its major partners in Oakland—described the action as a "frivolous, court-clogging lawsuit."

Within seconds, Davis took umbrage at his own remarks.

"That's slanderous!" cried the owner, cheeks tinting pink. "I have never advocated unwarranted litigation. This will not go unchallenged in court."

Davis then detailed his countersuit, which charges Davis with defamation of Davis's character, before leaving the room to confer with the Torts and

Rick Stewart/Getty Images Sport/Getty Images

Contracts unit of his 45-man legal team.

Asked to comment on the proceedings, the Raiders' head attorneys coach, Joe Alioto, seemed confused.

"Huh?" he said, slumping into a chair. "You want

me to discuss which now? Our grievance against the Oakland A's for underreporting billboard revenue? Our petition against the IRS? No? Then Al must be suing that referee from the tuck rule [2002 playoff] game. In that case, as in all cases, my client has no comment."

Head football coach Art Shell, the Raiders' highest-ranking non-attorney, was unavailable for comment. Sources said he was meeting with his staff to finalize the team's new 4–3 "Insanity" defense.

According to veteran Raiders official Al LoCasale, the bizarre episode began when Davis was preparing a grievance against the makers of Raid bug repellent for unauthorized use of most of the Raiders' name. With depositions barely underway and football season approaching, Davis abruptly demanded his offensive counsel "look into suing somebody new."

"To tell you the truth," said LoCasale, "I had to go through the phone book."

Although exhausted from studying game films and copyright law, Davis and his staff persevered. During a routine lunchtime evidence-gathering stroll, the owner noticed the Raiders' practice field was poorly maintained and the malpractice field even worse: Not one of the team's 38 paralegals hailed from a first-tier law school. Seeing this, Davis reflexively pulled a subpoena from his jacket pocket and began writing.

"With so much exciting smash-mouth Raiders litigation in the works," said LoCasale, "Al forgot that *he* was the party responsible for staffing and maintenance, and filed suit against himself."

Before terminating the interview, LoCasale defended his boss. "Listen, Al Davis's commitment to excellence is matched only by his commitment to exculpatory clauses."

"Mark my words," said Davis, before adjourning the press conference, "Once justice is served in this case, the Raiders and our fans will enjoy court-ordered stadium parking improvements, and refurbished grand and witness stands. Justice wins, baby!" ∎

WEB GEMS

We scour the Web so you don't have to

Our pick for the best sports item available this month.

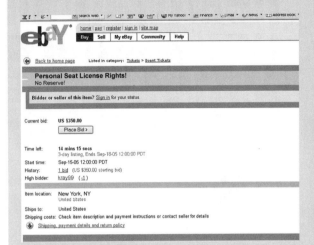

Personal Seat License Rights! No Reserve!

L@@k! Here it is! You can win the **opportunity to buy the opportunity to buy** a season ticket to the next home of the New York J . . . E . . . T . . . S Jets!Jets!Jets! Not an actual game ticket, your personal seat license grants you **a once-in-a-lifetime chance to pay in advance** for the rights to what may become **the hottest ticket in town!** Hopefully to be completed in 2009, the Jets' new state-of-the-art stadium may feature a retractable roof and only as many seats as will fit. Don't miss out!! In the past, seat licenses for **lousy expansion teams** have gone for **thousands of dollars.** This is for **Gang Green!** Why invest in a boring, lifeless piece of sports memorabilia when you can own a living, breathing **I.O.U!**

I'd love to keep it myself, but **ongoing family commitments** mean I can't. You can! **Buy the rights to my rights to buy** today!

Heartwarming, Fairy-Tale Win Fueled By Vicious Persecution Complex

Trailing by 28 points late in the third quarter, Cleveland Browns running back Ricky Cramer led his team on a gutsy comeback capped by a spectacular 17-yard touchdown run in double overtime. As party music rocked the stadium and the delirious home crowd danced in the seats and chanted his name after the winning play, Cramer appeared pleased and excited.

"Fuck all y'all!" he yelled to the crowd as he crossed the goal line, pounded his chest, and spiked the ball. "Y'all nothing but doubters and haters!"

As teammates mobbed the running back after his five-touchdown, 212-yard performance, Cramer pushed them away and pointed toward the heavens. "Hate on me all day, cut me down all week, you can't stop me," screamed Cramer at the press box.

"He's an amazing player, and he proves it time and time again," said TV analyst Richard Mark as cameras swept the giddy scene. "If there's one guy I'd want in my foxhole, it'd be Ricky. The consummate teammate."

While fans waved and shouted thanks to their hero, Cramer glared up at the luxury boxes. Inside, team officials were uncorking champagne in celebration of the franchise's first playoff berth in over a decade. "I spit on all y'all slave owners," he exclaimed, throwing his

"I can't wait to redo my contract and get the fuck out of here."

head back in derisive laughter and spitting on the grass.

"That was the most amazing come-from-behind win," said fan Nelson Scioli, still standing in his seat and clapping a full 10 minutes after the game had ended. "I mean, I never thought we'd come back from so far down! Ricky was a warrior out there, he's our heart and soul. I love him. Look—he's so overcome with joy, he's crying."

On the field below, Cramer had sunk to his knees, tears streaming down his face. "I can't wait to redo my contract and get the fuck out of here. And the fans—I'm just so happy that soon the fair-weather bloodsuckers who fill this shithole every week will have seen the last of number 47."

Despite winning a rushing title, earning millions in salary and bonuses, and legions of adoring fans—many of whom came to the game wearing Cramer jerseys—the running back remains sore over perceived slights from his rookie year five seasons ago.

"Everywhere I look and everywhere I go, I'm hearing motherfuckers tryin' to steal my flow," hissed

Cramer as he rushed through the otherwise euphoric locker room.

Later, as teammates made dinner plans, Cramer sat at his locker with headphones on and slowly peeled off his uniform, savoring the moment. Reading aloud from a yellowed newspaper clipping taped to the back of his locker, Cramer stared daggers around the room. The article, written during training camp five years ago, had gently questioned if, coming from a small college, the undersized fifth-round pick would be able to excel in the NFL.

"I got one thing to say to the press: Y'all can suck it."

"And to those 31 general managers who passed me up on draft day," said Cramer as he signed a football for an admirer in a wheelchair before departing alone, "HOW YOU LIKE ME NOW, HUH?" ∎

Nerf Polo Combines Nerf, Polo

Retailers and consumers are excited about Hasbro's Nerf Polo, to hit stores this holiday season.

"I tell them no, but my kids is always sneakin' some polo in the den," says mother of four Debra Lethan. "Last Christmas they broke two lamps and put a foot-long gash in the carpet. If they're serious about winnin' the Lancel Cup, now they can do it without tearin' up the house."

Priced at $34.95 a set, Nerf Polo is being promoted by Hasbro as a safe, nontoxic, equestrian alternative to popular rainy-day activities like board and video games.

Convenience is also a selling point, says polo dad Ross Milman. "Every time [daughter] Jill wanted to practice a nearside fore or a tail shot, we were off to Lancaster Stables, some 30 miles away. Not anymore. As long as Pepper, and Jill's friend's horses, all have their forelegs properly wrapped, they can just play upstairs."

Included in the set are three brightly colored balls made of patented Nerf foam, eight Nerf polo mallets, 32 Nerf horseshoes, and a plastic chukker timer. Horses are sold separately.

According to Randy Sheller, owner of Big Blue Toys in Walpole, Mass., advance sales have been promising. "I think Hasbro has hit a furniture-safe home run here. I'm getting calls about Nerf Polo every day. It is sure to do much better than last year's Nerf Clue, in which none of the characters could be killed."

Retired Deep Blue Artificially Contemplating Comeback

Once the biggest star in chess and an international celebrity, Deep Blue, IBM's most famous supercomputer, now spends its days in a cold warehouse basement, crunching numbers for the Brantley Insurance Co. and printing out copies of its own autograph to sell online. Those closest to the faded star say he is quietly training for another shot at the title.

At the IBM Training Compound in Southbury, Conn., Team Blue head programmer/sparring partner Murray Campbell discussed his longtime friend and protégé.

"It wasn't so long ago, DB was the biggest of the big," said Campbell, pointing with his cigar toward a framed 1997 photograph of Deep Blue with Vice President Al Gore, "Celebrity fund-raisers with Robin Williams, endorsement deals just pouring in through his internal fax . . . But that money is gone. He squandered it on a series of business ventures with Buster Douglas."

"He's too proud to say anything, but I know he's hurting," Campbell continued, his tone growing wistful. "Just a few years ago the guy was going one-on-one against [Gary] Kasparov with the

"But that money is gone. He squandered it on a series of business ventures with Buster Douglas."

whole world watching. And now he's part of a bank of 12 computers working on the same mundane database project, sharing this dingy little one-bedroom apartment with Max Headroom."

Deep Blue's professional inactivity gave rise to a personal inertia, one that saw his girlfriend, *Weird Science* star Kelly LeBrock, leave him just two years after his epic six-game defeat of Kasparov.

"Deep was fun at first," said LeBrock by telephone, "but once the cheering stopped, he sank into depression. He'd spend all day online, beating up chat-room chess opponents and incessantly Googling himself. Now I hear he's telling friends he's going to make a comeback? That would be a miracle. You know how this business is—you're over the hill once you turn four." ■

DEEP BLUE

Stay in School!!! Deep Blue '97 Champ 0101001

KASPAROV vs DEEP BLUE

ELECTRONIC ARTS LAUNCHES SENIORS GAMES

HEY, GRAMPA!

Tired of feeling left out? Just plain tired? Well, WAKE UP OLD MAN, because finally, the video game industry wants YOU. That's right! SwingStar Games has produced a line of titles designed expressly for YOU, THE COMPUTER-ILLITERATE RETIREE.

Super Mario 64 and Over is the perfect diversion to a day spent reading the newspaper and eating pudding. If that's too many barrels of simian mayhem for you, ramp it down with *Pokey Man.* Both have the intense 128-bit graphics craved by today's hottest gamers, but with storylines and pacing more suitable to someone on a pension and lots and lots of pills.

Seniors like yourself have more disposable income than teens and more sedentary lifestyles than adults, yet you've been completely overlooked by an entire wing of the entertainment industry. No longer! SwingStar games have been designed from the ground up for today's golden girls and boys.

Take our latest repurposed offering, *Grand Theft Auto: Advice City.* The notoriously risqué Las Vegas–style shoot-'em-up now takes place in Panama City, Fl. and features a white-haired driver sputtering along the breakdown lane in a 1991 Crown Victoria. As you hunt down and collar local miscreants in a palm-lined suburban setting, time-worn life lessons are imparted, in the voice of celebrity narrator Wilford Brimley.

If that's not your cup of decaf tea, than we have a slower, more bedridden adventure/mystery that begins inside a hospice facing a shortage of dialysis machines. *Gland Theft: Pinewood Knolls* is to be released in January.

But don't take our word for it—listen to a satisfied customer:

> "For years, the industry misunderstood the gaming needs of my generation. We grew up outside, playing ball, hiking, and just generally doing things. That makes us less likely to enjoy popular video games like *Final Fantasy XI: Chains of Promathia.* And for years, the choices for seniors were terrible: Virtual shuffleboard? The video knitting Activision released a few years ago? Please. *Golf Cart Simulator?* Give me a break. But *ABA Street,* featuring stars like Connie Hawkins playing half-court basketball, and *Lefty Grove Stickball?* Now you've got my attention."—Colba H., Laguna Woods, Calif.

Check with your physician to see if SwingStar Games are right for you.

Red Sox Victims Of Latest Reality Hit, *So You Think You've Won The World Series?*

Real World Series to start next month

The Boston Red Sox and their millions of devoted fans were treated to a delicious surprise last Saturday: Instead of a victory parade, the Red Sox were greeted at City Hall by a Fox production team and the actors who played the roles of the St. Louis Cardinals in the "World Series."

The Red Sox had been punk'd.

The concept of *So You Think You've Won the World Series?* was modeled on the wildly successful hoodwinking of Al Gore in 2000's *The Presidency: Whoomp! There It Ain't.*

After Boston won two miraculous extra-inning games against the Yankees in the American League Championship Series, says producer Len Rominick, "you sensed they had the momentum and might actually pull it off. That's when I first got the idea for a hoax World Series, and approached Commissioner Selig. He loved the commercial potential of a staged finale, and so I immediately started auditioning Cardinals look-alikes.

"Knowing the decades of agony surrounding this franchise,

and the way their fans get tied up in emotional knots every time the team gets close—it just seemed like the perfect setup for a great joke, one that America wanted to hear."

Rominick, producer of such reality sensations as *The "Fun" in Funeral* and *Who Wants to Perform Fellatio on a Congressman?,* said the biggest challenge was finding actors who resembled the real Cardinals and could "reasonably simulate" Major League play.

The cover was nearly blown as the "Cardinals" were strikingly inept in virtually every facet of the game, never leading at any moment in the Series.

Told that the four-game sweep was in fact staged for a national TV audience, a champagne-soaked and sleep-deprived Curt Schilling punched Fox correspondent Melanie Feuer in the face. *So You Think You've Won the World Series?* drew an overnight 18.2 rating, with an impressive 32 percent share.

After watching their team win a Major League–high 105 games this year, Cardinals fans could be forgiven for being suspicious.

"It was hard not to notice that Jim Edmonds and Scott Rolen were both swinging the bat like little leaguers," said Rick Posnett, 26, of St. Louis, "And when Jeff Suppan did that ridiculous dance move off of third base I said, 'Who's that actor impersonating a major leaguer?' But I was just kidding around."

Or so he thought.

Said Rominick, "Some of the best reality TV is based on the premise that people want to be surprised, and manipulated, even if they don't realize it. Like *Joe Millionaire*—those women didn't really want to marry a rich guy; they wanted the shock of falling for the working-class hunk he turned out to be. And the same is true of Red Sox fans: They don't truly want victory; they want hope growing bit by bit into belief, and then utter devastation at the fin-ish line. And that's what we've given them."

Confirming this was Posnett, who said that the 3 million Sox fans who turned out for the victory parade, only to learn that their long-coveted championship was nothing more than a television stunt, "actually seemed relieved." ■

THIS MONTH IN HISTORY
December 21, 1933
In first attempt to gain better traction in cold conditions, New York Giants don snowshoes, lose to Lions 54-3.

December 4, 1968
To win back fans after recent "Heidi game" mishap, NBC interrupts *The Sound of Music* with two minutes of Jets highlights.

AIRWAVES
Where we spotlight those who talk about those who do

Carl Herschwood, who spent six years researching the George Brett "pine tar game" for his book Crime Against Humanity, *was recently hired by ESPN for its Monday Night Football broadcasts. Following are excerpts from his first game on the job.*

Carl Herschwood, Sideline Investigative Reporter Panthers/Jaguars, December 6, Jacksonville DISPATCHES

9:03 P.M. EST: Hmm. Everyone's tight-lipped down here, Al and John. I'm going to have to pour some drinks.

9:14: Guys, I have it on deep background that Panthers coach John Fox might have a nanny problem. Back to you.

9:27: I can't reveal my sources, Al, but let's just say a certain trick play commonly associated with an insect just might be attempted tonight by the Jags.

9:33: Hi again, folks! Next quarter I'll be embedded with the Panthers' offensive line.

9:43: I've got three eyewitnesses corroborating that Julius Peppers is walking with a limp. Groin pull?

10:11: Hi, folks. I'm whispering because I'm under the Jags bench, poking around Fred Taylor's bleeding calf. Official reports are false: seems like more than a bruise.

10:20: Al, I talked with Coach Del Rio just before the half. Unfortunately, it will have to remain off the record.

10:33: Well, I finally nabbed Steve Smith for a sit-down after his big catch. The nut of it is, he was excited.

10:47: Insiders granted your humble newsy here covert access to the Panthers' playbook, Al. It's quite a dossier. I can say with impunity that, at this juncture, not everything has proceeded according to plan.

11:15: Earlier reports that Jake Delhomme called the cameraman a "homo" are not credible. I reviewed the tape; he said, "Hi, mom."

Finally, Somebody Stood Up And Cold-Cocked The Fans

BY J. B. GALISHAW

About freakin' time. This ain't the Ice Capades, this is basketball. It's rough. It's tough. At any moment an opposing player can charge up the aisle a dozen rows, push three people out of the way, and swift-kick a size-18 Converse into your jaw.

That's just part of the game. You know it and I know it.

But what I don't know is why it has to be shown over and over again on the *Today* show. What's the big deal? Shelling out a few hundred bucks for a courtside seat doesn't mean the employees can't put

These whining NBA apparel-wearing fans are such prima donnas.

their hands on you. I've seen magicians take people out of the crowd and saw them in half, yet you never hear a word against it from Matt Lauer.

Look, basketball players work their butts off 82 days a year, sometimes even more. A few swings at the back of your head is not too much to ask in return.

The problem is the fans.

Always clapping. Reading the program. Buying $5 sodas. Why shouldn't they have to drive home

holding ice packs to their bruised necks?

These whining NBA apparel-wearing fans are such prima donnas. The moms, the dads, the little girls with the team jerseys. Each and every one of them deserves a fist-shaped wakeup call from a 7-foot center. Especially the corporate types sitting down low. They have no right to complain when their Kenneth Coles are stepped on by players rushing up to sucker-punch other fans.

And another thing, if that's me getting waled on by the Defensive Player of the Year, I'm cool with it! News flash: That ain't no scrub crumpling the cartilage in your nose—that's a bona fide superstar. You're getting the autograph of a lifetime. Relax and enjoy it.

Players today have busy lives. Pressure-packed. But even with all the other responsibilities that command their personal time—sneaker commercials, chrome dubs, drum loops—these guys make it to the arena by tipoff to sweat for you.

In conclusion: Just because your ticket helps pay a power forward's eight-figure salary doesn't mean he shouldn't punch you in the face. ∎

J. B. Galishaw is our senior editor and the author of Four Quarters (Make Me Wanna Dollar): Memoirs of an NBA Season Ticket Holder.

Emergency Statement of Apology

It is with great regret/shame/contractual obligations that I appear before you all today.

As you may know, while under the influence of alcohol/Vicodin/Ray Lewis, I may have said/done/punched some things which I probably should not have. Even though my comments/actions/wife were taken out of context/in self-defense/okay with it, if anyone was offended/hurt/impregnated by them, I apologize.

I am confident that the league/law/corporate sponsors will find me innocent of all charges and that justice/truth/the ol' boys' network will prevail.

It is my sincere/profound/agent's hope that all of my fans/groupies/illegitimate offspring can put this unfortunate incident/trial/triple homicide behind them and focus on the task at hand: winning the NBA Finals/Super Bowl/World Series of Poker for all the people of Portland/Oakland/color.

I will not be taking any questions/ecstasy/contraceptives from the media/coaches/fans at this time. The main thing right now is that I'm just trying to stay focused/positive/in school.

Finally, I only hope that I can learn/grow/profit from this regrettable/tragic/carefully-orchestrated-CD-marketing event. Thank you all very much.

Cut along dotted line and keep in your wallet.

ABOUT THE AUTHORS

Ken Widmann and Dan Appel are the comedy-writing team behind the sports satire website SayItAintSo.com.

Ken's writing has appeared in various publications, including *The OC Weekly*, *The Fairfield County Weekly*, and *The Onion*. A former teacher, he holds a B.A. in history from Connecticut College and an M.A. in American civilization from Brown University. He and his wife, Janet, live in Northern California.

Dan Appel grew up in Manhattan and lives in Brooklyn. He graduated from Harvard with a degree in anthropology; while in college he was a researcher/writer for the *Let's Go USA* and *Let's Go California* travel books.

Dave Lehman works for Autonomy Inc. as a software sales manager. He holds a B.S. in mechanical engineering, with a focus on design, from M.I.T.